PRAISE FOR THE ART OF COACHING CLERGY

"My respected coaching colleague Rev. Chris Holmes writes in the same way he speaks: with clarity, curiosity, and compassion. In *The Art of Coaching Clergy*, Chris does a brilliant job explaining professional coaching both generally and in its applications to coaching of and by clergy. I highly recommend Chris's book to people interested in coaching regardless of their faith."

—Ed Modell, JD, PCC
past president, International Coach Federation

"How does one learn the practice of ministry? How does one learn to be authentically oneself when others expect a particular role? How does one learn what cannot be taught? Ministry, by both clergy and laity, is complex and unique and must be learned in the setting where it happens. Chris is the voice of one who has trained and practiced being the conversation partner, the coach, who walks alongside leaders who must find their own paths. His book is a proposal for a healthy way forward, less distracted by the 'experts' and more open to the Spirit."

—Gil Rendle, denominational consultant and author of *Journey in the Wilderness* and *Doing the Math of Mission*

"Having Chris Holmes train clergy coaches is a sight to behold. Here is the next best thing: his handbook on coaching, *The Art of Coaching Clergy*. He makes the case for why coaching is so important to not only the effectiveness of clergy, but also to their faithfulness and spiritual and emotional health. After reading this handbook, you might just want to get some coaching yourself."

—Bishop Scott Benhase,
bishop of the Episcopal Diocese of Georgia

"My friend and colleague Chris Holmes is a courageous pioneer in clergy coaching. *The Art of Coaching Clergy* is a gift to leaders in their pursuit to bring out the best in others. Through an understanding that we all are creative, resourceful, and whole, Chris leads us on an adventure of discovering and enhancing leaders' soul through key coaching concepts and powerful questions, stories, and examples of leadership. A must-read for leaders who want to coach up leaders, congregations, and organizations."

—Bishop John Schol, bishop of the Greater New Jersey Annual Conference of the United Methodist Church

"Chris Holmes clergy coaching handbook illuminates what coaching is and what it is not. He brings clarity to the discipline and its impact on holistic living for clergy. Coaching, as Chris describes it, is not just a technique, but a spiritual practice for the pastor as a way of being and interacting with the world.

"Consider *The Art of Coaching Clergy* necessary reading for those who are considering engaging a coach or for those who want to go deeper in their own work as coaches.

—**Rev. Dr. Phil Schroeder**, director of congregational development, North Georgia Conference of the United Methodist Church

THE ART OF COACHING CLERGY

A HANDBOOK FOR CHURCH LEADERS, CLERGY, AND COACHES

REV. CHRIS HOLMES

ISBN 13: 978-1717143976

ISBN-10: 1717143970

Interior design by Kristen Otte

Cover design by Taylor Holmes

Edited by Candace Johnson, Change It Up Editing

Scripture quoted in this book is from the New Revised Standard Version of the Bible (NRSV), unless otherwise noted. Other Bible versions include The Message (MSG), New International Version (NIV), and New American Standard Version (NASV).

To my wife, Margaret—by far the most vivaciously alive, curious, and naturally coach-like person I have ever met.

CONTENTS

FOREWORD

In 2008, Reverend Chris Holmes and I had a dream of a culture of coaching within the United Methodist Church in the United States, and then we heard God ask, "Why not within other denominations?" and then "Why not globally?" Step by step, the dream became a plan that God has blessed into becoming an astounding reality. We have not only steered the birth of a large-scale coaching movement within the United Methodist Church in the United States, but also in other denominations, and more recently in parts of Africa and Europe.

As the Executive Director of Global Coaching for the UMC's Global Mission agency, I have the privilege of identifying and equipping emerging coaches at Africa University in Zimbabwe. The team of coaches is developing a culture of coaching at the university that incorporates students from twenty-eight different African countries. Identifying leaders and equipping them with coaching skills has been a part of my work for the past fifteen years.

Our journey as coaches began in different settings: Chris's as a United Methodist pastor and district superintendent in the Baltimore-Washington area, and mine as director of congregational development for the United Methodist Church in West Ohio. The journeys converged one day as we sat in kayaks circling one another on Lake Junaluska in North Carolina and discovered each other's dreams for supporting and empowering pastors and leaders. Soon after, we received a request from Discipleship Ministries of the UMC to design and lead a national coach training seminar for denominational leaders.

The pilot was a success. The seeds were planted, and thousands of pastors, laity, and denominational leaders have since been trained using our "Coach Approach Skill Training" curriculum. A number are now certified by the International Coach Federation.

The Art of Coaching Clergy is about pastors and laypeople turning their dreams into goals and their goals into reality. It is a timely reflection on leadership and a key approach to increasing the capacity of Christians to fulfill their calling as leaders.

These pages read like a handbook written specifically for pastors and their leadership. It is for church leaders who are seeking to make a difference and willing to invest the effort to realize a new reality for their church and ministry. It is designed with pastors and laypeople in mind and is applicable in a wide variety of cultures and contexts. It is also helpful for leaders in judicatory positions whose desire is to come alongside leaders in their circle of influence to encourage them to be their best selves.

Life by its very nature is change. One day often resembles the next, yet we are older, stronger, fatter, more hopeful, or more confused than the day before. We face political, economic, and cultural shifts in our own lives, the church, and society at large. The question is how we meet the change with great courage and empower other leaders to do the same.

It is here that coaching makes considerable impact. Coaches prod, encourage, and empower pastors toward self-discovery. We assist the process of digging deep into a person's own experience, knowledge, capabilities, and understanding of the context to clarify and articulate his or her own goals and action plans. We help pastors stay committed to the strategic and important over the immediate and often unimportant. Over time these action plans along with their own accountability systems move these leaders to a new reality.

We have worked with leaders seeking bold change in their own leadership as well is in the churches, communities, cities, states, and denominations in which they serve. These leaders are committed to the transformation of individuals and communities one life and one system at a time. They are not simply trying to tweak a process or a structure, but are seeking ways in which the message of hope is more clearly seen and people and communities are transformed.

Having coached hundreds of such leaders moving through change, Reverend Chris Holmes offers compelling insights into both the practice of coaching and its results. *The Art of Coaching Clergy* offers serious exploration of biblical and theological foundations for coaching as well as astute practical applications of coaching and peer coaching systems as a means of transformation in ministry. Perhaps more than anyone, Chris has helped shape the contours of the art of clergy coaching in the last ten years, proving him to be a foremost thought leader in this field. It is from this vantage point he offers *The Art of Coaching Clergy* as a generous gift to leaders and the coaching movement.

—George Howard, PCC
Executive director of global coaching, UMC Global Ministries

PREFACE

Clergy tend to be skeptical about the latest and greatest thing to come along, and rightfully so. Those who have been in ministry for a while have lived through several versions of strategic planning, organizational goal setting, mission statement development, and vision casting. Few of these efforts have proven to lead to significant transformation.

So, in coaching clergy, the initial hurdle to overcome is a weariness and resistance to what is sometimes introduced as the next great thing that will save us. Coaching is not the panacea that will save congregations or dwindling denominations, but it has proven to consistently strengthen clergy leadership, which affords greater clarity and courageous action.

Clergy coaching is not a quick fix.

It is not a program.

It is not a package or curriculum.

It is not a course or a production.

It is not a strategic plan or a blue print.

It is not a syllabus or a formula.

Coaching is a relationship!

Coaching is an intentional affiliation that is highly personal, deeply intentional, and always contextual. The only "agency" coaching has is genuine relationship.

Since 2010, the number of professional coaches coaching pastors, denominational leaders, and congregations has tripled. This is just the beginning of an impressive bell curve of growth in the use of coaches for clergy in the coming years.

This handbook is written to help shape the field of leadership in the church today through the lens of coaching, stir ideas about the beneficial applications of coaching in the work of ministry, and add biblical and theological depth to the underpinnings of coaching.

In these pages, we resolutely call forth a coach-like, artful style of church leadership …

- that is less top down and more come alongside.
- that listens more and tells less.
- that asks great questions rather than giving okay answers.
- that honors resourcefulness while daring to expect accountability.
- that recognizes church leaders as the experts in their settings.
- that co-creates a vision for the future.
- that mines a leader's experience and knowledge in creating action plans.

People who will benefit from reading this book are church leaders, those who coach clergy, people who are exploring the call to become a coach, those who are being coached, those responsible for the development of clergy leadership, denominational leaders, and all people who are simply curious about the power and mystique of the clergy coaching relationship.

Incidentally, this book is *about coaching*; it is not an instructional manual that teaches the skills of coaching. While I do introduce some basic coaching techniques, I focus more on the variety of ways to apply the modality of coaching to the work of ministry. The actual skills of coaching are best learned by attending one of the coach training courses that has been certified by the International Coach Federation. More information about the Coach Approach Skill Training for ministry can be found in the appendix at the back of this book or on our website, www.holmescoaching.com.

————

Part One of this handbook paints a basic understanding of coaching clergy.

Part Two is more of the "how to" portion of this book and will be of most help to people interested in hiring a coach, becoming a coach, or exploring what life as a clergy coach looks like.

Part Three surveys a variety of specific applications of coaching in working with clergy in the church today, while Part Four focuses on coaching ministry systems.

In each chapter, you will encounter noteworthy contributors to the subject of the chapter under the rubric *Ruminations*. According to English Oxford Living Dictionary, rumination is literally "A deep or considered thought about something."[1] There is intentional gender, ethnicity, age, and theological diversity in this collection of leaders who offer their unique perspectives on coaching for you to mull over and digest.

Whether you are clergy, lay, a denominational leader, or some other intrepid spiritual nomad, in these pages you will find a clear picture of the art of coaching clergy.

Notes

1. English Oxford Living Dictionary, s.v. *"rumination,"* accessed April 03, 2018, https://en.oxforddictionaries.com/definition/rumination.

INTRODUCTION

Counselors and spiritual directors, mentors, and consultants have been helpful to pastors and congregations for many years. These original four well-established helping professions are not quite sure what to make of the flashy red-headed cousin called "coaching," who is the most recent profession to pull up a stool and join the table of helping ministries.

On the one hand, its profile does seem to share the family resemblance: helpful, authoritative, and client-centered. However, on the other hand, considering its young age, coaching may also appear rather bold—too attention-seeking, curious, inquisitive, and ill-defined for its own good—perhaps even a little annoying.

There is good reason to be suspicious. Once upon a time, anybody could call himself or herself a coach. The sprouting coaching movement of the 1970s was so loosely defined and unregulated that it had a credibility problem. People interested in herbal remedies overnight emerged as "herbalist coaches," and tarot card readers with no coach training donned the title "life coach." The now-reputable vocation of coaching is still trying to recover from its flake-factor roots.

Coaching is still trying to recover from its flake-factor roots.

Largely due to the efforts of the International Coach Federation (ICF), which was founded in 1995, the field of coaching has grown into a respectable global profession. Coaches today are credentialed, which means they must meet certain education requirements, obtain qualified mentor coaching, submit a specified number of client coaching hours, and pass a coach knowledge assessment exam. They must also adhere to a comprehensive professional Code of Ethics.

The field of coaching has grown into a respectable global profession.

Today, most trained coaches specialize in a particular realm of coaching, such as health and wellness, retirement, business, employment, transitioning, or executive coaching to name a few. Each of these are sub-specialties that fall under the broad umbrella labeled "life coaching." A growing number of professional coaches are now applying these basic skills to the transformation of the lives of individuals and church organizations. As the practice of coaching matures, clergy coaching will progressively "take up space" at the table of helping professions, and its voice will grow stronger.

The Clergy Coaching Stance in Relation to Other Helping Professions

Coaching is not better than the other cousins; however, coaches do take a different posture toward the work of helping. Much like a surfer on a surfboard, or a golfer getting ready to swing the club, or a baseball player positioned for the pitch in the batters box, the beginning "stance" taken in relationship to the client is absolutely critical. The stance we take in coaching is different from each of the other helping modalities. To clearly understand this uniqueness, we must take a quick look at some of the underlying assumptions driving the first four helping modalities.

Counseling

The opening stance in counseling is "helping with brokenness." Most people go to a counselor for assistance in resolving problematic behavior, beliefs, feeling or relationships. The therapeutic model begins with what is not working in a person's life and very often the source of their pain. The expertise lies with the clinician who diagnoses and treats the patient.

Coaching differs from counseling, in that we do not begin by diagnosing and classifying a person's mental disorder according to "The Diagnostic and Statistical Manual of Mental Disorders" (DSM), and directing our focus to the brokenness in their lives.

Counseling is an important helping modality, but it is not coaching.

Spiritual Direction

The stance of a spiritual director is "exploratory companion" on a person's path of spiritual growth. Spiritual direction focuses on an individual's relationship with God and his or her growth in personal spirituality. The director may ask questions about a person's prayer life or experience of God in life.

Spiritual direction is a vital discipline, and perhaps the closest cousin to coaching, but spiritual direction is not coaching. A coach will be more focused on the action steps the person being coached would like to take concerning that person's spiritual life, and also how that individual wants to be held accountable.

Mentoring

The stance taken by a mentor is usually that of "wise elder." The mentor relates to the person being mentored from a place of knowing. Mentors typically have a body of experience to draw from and to share with others. The person being mentored is expected to bring the questions and do most of the listening, while the mentor has the answers and does most of the talking.

Mentoring is a crucial form of helping, but mentoring is not coaching.

Consulting

The key words in the stance of a consultant are "expert" and "advice." A consultant is hired to provide expert advice to a company or individual for an established fee. The consultant's voice is usually from outside the system or organization.

Many individuals and organizations have found consultants to be helpful, but consulting is not coaching.

Where Coaching Begins

We begin with an individual's amazing resilience, believing each person is tremendously capable, wonderfully insightful, gifted, and competent. This is our bedrock conviction: the person being coached is "naturally creative, resourceful, and whole."[1]

We discover how a person is currently experiencing his or her life or ministry and then help that individual glance forward rather than backward. We are curious—not about why things are the way they are, but what needs to be different going forward to realize the client's vision for his or her future. We do not avoid a person's past, but our questions are more around the God-sized things wanting to emerge in the person's life as we probe the future that person is moved to create.

An example of the power of coaching is found in this statement, which was recently shared in a coaching cohort: "I have made more progress after only a few coaching sessions helping me to explore my possibilities than I have in seven years of therapy obsessing about my past."

Coaches are fiercely committed to each person's capability and magnificence. Our role is not to take care of or "play small" with the people we coach. At times, we even hold this irrefutably favorable view of them when they stop believing it about themselves. We stand in the gap committed to their wholeness. The theology around the perspective of wholeness is significant enough that we will explore it in greater depth in Chapter 3.

Coaches are fiercely committed to each person's capability and magnificence.

Where the Expertise Lies

As we discussed above, mentors are experts who share their experience from a place of knowing, and consultants give expert advice. In both cases the expertise lies with the giver. The coaching stance is radically different, in that we believe each person we interact with is the expert on his or her own life. It would be impossible to overemphasize the absolute foundational nature of this conviction.

In coaching we know that the expertise that really matters lies within the person being coached.

We believe that the people we are coaching already possess the deep inner wisdom needed to create options, make decisions, and devise outstanding plans, so our job becomes helping them excavate that gold by listening deeply, staying curious, exploring alternatives, and asking good questions. The client may feel stuck or confused about what to do or may have settled into unhealthy routines, but the only person who can bring the needed discernment, genius, and willpower to make a change is the person being coached.

Instead of seeing ourselves as experts in someone else's life, conversationally coaches see ourselves as partners. We come alongside the individuals we coach, metaphorically "shoulder to shoulder" with them on their journey of self-discovery.

Advice and the Brain

We now know from brain science that advice being given by another person appeals mostly to the rational parts of the other person's brain and does not actually embed in the neocortex, the part of the brain involved in higher functions such as sensory perception, spatial reasoning, conscious thought, and in humans, language. The brain of the person hearing advice actually goes into neutral, which means they are less likely to take ownership of advice offered.[2]

Pastors are tired of being told what to do by someone outside the congregation who does not fully understand their ministry setting in all of its uniqueness. Pastors most often follow through with blueprints they draft rather than those handed down to them by others.

Pastors are tired of being told what to do by someone outside the congregation who does not fully understand their ministry setting.

A good coach will resist the temptation to make suggestions, share their experience, and offer solutions, even though they may indeed have good suggestions, helpful experience, and reasonable solutions. Instead, coaches "manage their own brilliance," knowing that to give advice is to rob the person being coached of coming up with his or her own insights and plans, which shortcuts the leadership development required to build their capacity.

Regardless of your starting point in understanding coaching, or the modality you are most familiar with in the helping professions, in the following pages you will find an introduction to and an exploration of coaching as a leadership art form. We will also explore the application of coaching in a variety of group and individual ministry settings.

Notes

1. Henry Kimsey-House, Karen Kimsey-House, Phillip Sandahl, and Laura Whitworth, *CoActive Coaching: Changing Business Transforming Lives*, 3rd edition (Boston, MA: Nicholas Brealey Publishing, 2011), 3–4.
2. David Rock, "A Brain-Based Approach to Coaching," *International Journal of Coaching in Organizations*, 2006, 4(2), 42.

PART I

UNDERSTANDING CLERGY COACHING

UNDERSTANDING CLERGY COACHING: ARCHEOLOGY OF THE SOUL

I was once a member of an archeological team surveying unexcavated ruins in the hills of central Mexico. We uncovered broken clay pots, tools, and obsidian fragments which were then carbon-dated and examined for clues about the life and culture of the Mayan people.

Archeology is the scientific study of past human life and culture by the examination of physical remains such as graves, tools, and pottery. But even more paramount, archeology is an adventure, a discovery, an investigative quest. It is a wondering, a following of hunches driven by curiosity to see what can be revealed.

Think of coaching as the *art of purposeful conversation applied to the archeology of the soul*.

Coaching is an unearthing process, not of a buried ruin, but of a living soul who is willing to explore his or her burgeoning potential. Digging is a part of the process ... only our digging tools are not a trowel, shovel, and brush, but questions, curiosity, and conversation. Our focus of discovery in not what once was, but of what can be. We focus not on what happened, but on what is happening, what is possible, and the action those lead to.

> Think of coaching as the *art of purposeful conversation applied to the archeology of the soul.*

Tenacious Curiosity

One of the proficiencies we develop in coaching is a tenacious sense of curiosity. It helps us stay present to the person we are coaching and to continually delve deeper in conversation. We are actually recovering a gift that came naturally to us at a much younger age.

If you've ever been on a walk with a five-year-old, you know she will find many interesting things along the way. If there is a bug on the sidewalk, she will poke it. If the leaves are pretty, she will collect them. According to a paper presented at the 2012 Global Summit held by the International Coaching Federation,

> A five-year-old on average engages in 98 creative tasks per day. By contrast, a 44-year-old engages in two creative tasks per day. A 5-year-old on average laughs 113 times per day; a 44-year-old laughs 11 times. A 5-year-old on average asks 65 questions per day; 44-year-olds ask four.

I believe curiosity is one of the values Jesus had in mind when he said, "Truly, I say to you, unless you turn and become like children, you will never enter the kingdom of heaven" (Mt 18:3 NIV). Coaches probe with insatiable inquisitiveness, push beyond surface reflection, and question the obvious. We dare to poke the bug.

Coaches stay curious throughout a coaching conversation by quieting their own inner voices and asking exploratory questions from a place of deep listening. We inquire about the details of a person's story and what it means to him or her with questions like "Tell me more about that," "Let's explore that at a deeper level," and "Please share more about what that was like for you."

Coaches probe with insatiable inquisitiveness, push beyond surface reflection, and question the obvious.

In the study of the Bible, *exegesis* is the process of carefully drawing out the meaning of a sacred text according to its context and the author's intended meaning. *Eisegesis* occurs when the reader interjects his or her own interpretation into a text, therefore making the words say what the reader wants.

Much of the listening the average person does in daily life is akin to *eisegesis* of biblical study. In other words, we ascribe our own judgments and meaning to a story being told to us rather than asking questions to draw out the meaning the story holds for the person who is sharing it. The true essence of a story is the meaning it holds for the storyteller.

For good coaches, curiosity is our *exegesis*. It becomes the exploratory driver to help reveal the significance and implication of what is being communicated in a conversation. We do our best to suspend judgment and resist the urge to impose our own interpretation. We listen to others the way Mark Nepo describes "the way veins listen to blood."[1]

Curiosity is our exegesis.

Through the coach's stance of curiosity, those being coached will unravel new options to consider and see additional possibilities that may not have been obvious before.

Encouragement

Pastoring a congregation has become increasingly challenging work, and it is driving a significant number of pastors to consider doing something else professionally. In fact, one study completed by the Fuller Institute in 1998 claims that "over 70% of pastors are so stressed out and burned out that they regularly consider leaving the ministry."[2] That is a chilling statistic. Many pastors feel a sense of *vocational checkmate* because it is difficult for them to imagine their skills being transferable to other kinds of work.

Coaching has helped countless pastors reconnect with the original call God placed on their lives and find a meaningful way forward— a way to not just stick it out in ministry, but to thrive. Being heard, supported, and encouraged from the coaching stance has a tremendous impact. We help leaders figure out what to do next. Coaching helps pastors apply skills and experience in their current ministry, new settings in pastoral ministry, and other contexts outside of ministry.

A coach champions the person being coached when nobody else does. A coach points out that person's brilliance, lifts up his or her accomplishments, and celebrates the individual's successes. At times, coaches hold their coaching clients bigger than those clients may feel at the moment, and we remind them of their wholeness, their resourcefulness, and their God-giftedness. The coaching stance is one of authentic and truthful encouragement.

Time for Action

Another important part of the coaching stance, and one not necessarily shared by the other helping modalities, is the strong push for action. Coaches always aim to end coaching sessions with commitment to action. Like many people, pastors tend to be better at talking about what needs to be done than they are at following through with actually doing those things. Theologian Henry Nouwen says, "Spiritual maturity is not knowing what to do with your whole life, but what to do next."[3] So a good coach will predictably ask this trinity of questions:

- "What are you committing to do?"
- "When will you do it?"
- "How would you like to be held accountable?"

"Spiritual maturity is not knowing what to do with your whole life, but what to do next."

—HENRY NOUWEN

Church leaders have shelves of books on leadership, congregational growth, five easy steps to … whatever. They have read those books, highlighted and underlined them, and put them right back on their shelves. They have another few shelves lined with folders, binders, and notebooks from conferences they've attended. Those books and conferences were helpful and interesting, but the amount of action taken in ministry generated by that material is nowhere close to matching the extent of bookshelf real estate the material occupies.

Perhaps most of us have read enough on leadership.

Perhaps we have invested enough time in workshops and seminars.

Perhaps we have attended enough week-long seminars at large churches to learn how they do ministry in their setting.

Perhaps we are looking for wisdom in all the wrong places.

Where is the evidence of action leading to transformational change in individual lives and congregations resulting from all that investment?

Most of the answers we seek are not out there in a book or found at a seminar. Ministry is not that simple. The answers to the way forward in ministry lie within each clergy leader working closely with lay leadership under God's shaping. Coaching is the powerful means to help excavate those answers as leaders tap their deep inner wisdom stirred up by the Holy Spirit.

The answers to the way forward in ministry lie within each clergy leader working closely with lay leadership.

Christian coaches Linda Miller and Chad Hall express it well.

> The answer to, "What's next?" is no longer evident by examining past successes. In such a context, Christian coaching is an appropriate response because it enables one to relate to others not as an expert who knows the way from experience, but as a partner who can help discover the way.[4]

One objective of coaching is to help the person being coached sort through the morass of conscious and subconscious thoughts, feelings, and ideas, design a path forward, and take action. We do this by helping the pastor or layperson tune in to his or her own voice at a volume greater than the other voices. An individual's own deep-seated wisdom becomes the organizing authority where clarity is found.

For some, this inner wisdom is the same as trusting their intuition or following their gut. After all, the brain and the gut have substantially the same metaphysical makeup, which is why the gut is sometimes referred to as the "second brain." Often, we feel something in our gut before we discern it in our head.

People of faith believe there is another dimension to this trusting of the gut. We believe the gut to also be the locale of spiritual discernment from which we listen to God's voice, experience the confirming nudge of the spirit, or search out divine guidance. The Quakers refer to this spiritual confirmation or clarity regarding what action to take as "a way opening." When a way opens, obstacles and resistance seem to dissipate, and a path forward emerges.

The resulting action carries the insignia of the leader's own personal authority and also the authority of the Holy Spirit. In the end, the action may not turn out to be the best, but utilizing all the decision-maker has to go on at the time, it is, in fact, the best decision.

We believe the gut is also the locale of spiritual discernment from which we listen to God's voice.

It Is God's Work

Very often what happens in coaching is transformational; lives are changed, ministries are refocused, and congregations move forward. At times, the courageous work pastors have done has taken my breath away. This is gratifying work, but coaching is an illusion if self-credited by the coach.

From our lens of faith, the clergy coach is utterly clear that we are not the ones bringing about change in the life of someone else. It is the person being coached who brings about that change with God's help. The Holy Spirit is at work in the relationship.

Andre Gide, the twentieth-century French author and winner of the Nobel Prize in Literature, said, "Art is a collaboration between God and the artist, and the less the artist does the better."[5] A similar principle is at work in coaching. What happens in coaching is a three-way collaboration between God, the person being coached, and the coach, with the coach being the least causative factor. Life transformation really is a God thing.

Coaching is a three-way collaboration between God, the person being coached, and the coach, with the coach being the least causative factor.

As a Christian coach, I trust that the transformation occurring in a person's life is the work of the Holy Spirit and is the outcome God would have for him or her. Because I trust that God is ostensibly present in the transformative work of coaching, I trust God with the process and the outcome of the coaching. This elemental belief keeps me from the temptation to bend the coaching to make it seem more outwardly religious or to force the use of faith language or reference the familiar context of my tradition as the portal for change. It also keeps me from interposing my agenda.

Ironically, agenda-driven Christian coaching may undermine the very life transformation that is possible for the person being coached by restrictively shaping the container for that transformation to occur. It also limits a coach's opportunity to engage with people who are "church-adverse" or wary of organized religion.

Trusting the open container of the coaching relationship and the work of the ever-present Holy Spirit is a powerful means for life transformation. Coaching is spiritual work every time I engage with a client, regardless of that client's religious affiliation, beliefs, or awareness. The focus of coaching is not just a person's "doing," but also about that person's "being." To coach from this perspective makes coaching not just spiritual; it is, in fact, the holiest vocation I can think of.

Notes

1. Mark Nepo, *Seven Thousand Ways to Listen: Staying Close to What Is Sacred* (New York, Free Press, 2014), 14.
2. Richard J. Krejcir, "Francis Schaeffer Statistics on Pastors," accessed March 18, 2018, http://www.intothyword.org/apps/articles/default.asp?articleid=36562&columnid=3958.
3. Henry Nouwen, last accessed March 18, 2018, http://www.azquotes.com/quote/1457936..
4. Linda J. Miller and Chad W. Hall, *Coaching for Christian Leaders: A Practical Guide*, (St. Louis: Chalice Press, 2007), 2.
5. Heather Wagoner, "The Science of Listening," *The Huffington Post*, July 17, 2017, https://www.huffingtonpost.com/heather-wagoner/the-science-of-listening_b_11030950.html.

2

BIBLICAL FOUNDATIONS FOR COACHING

The holy vocation of coaching is deeply rooted in the biblical narrative of the Christian faith recorded in both the Hebrew scriptures and the New Testament. While numerous corollaries to coaching can be found in scripture, I have selected examples and stories from the Gospels of Matthew, Mark, Luke, and John, as well as Exodus, 1 Samuel, and the Book of Romans.

Jesus As a Coach-Like Leader

The Jesus we see represented consistently in scripture is a teaching rabbi who told stories, taught Torah, and asked disconcerting questions.

Jesus told a parable and would then generally ask the disciples or the crowd what it meant to them. He required listeners to apply his teaching to their own lives. At times of frustration he would sometimes expound upon the story, but mostly he left the application up to the listener.

The most coach-like part of Jesus' teaching style were the kinds of questions he asked. His questions were jarring and would elicit either silence or deeper thinking, and his direct communication challenged inconsistencies and falsehoods.

The most coach-like part of Jesus' teaching style were the kinds of questions he asked.

The Question of Great Substance

In the beginning of John's Gospel when the Messiah appears, he does not begin with a sermon; he opens his ministry with an enormous question to the two representative disciples, Andrew and Simon Peter. He asked them, "What do you want?" (Jn 1:38 NIV).

This question, in a variety of forms, is the foundational question for all coaching.

What do you want …

- from life?
- to be different?
- to accomplish this year?
- to change in your ministry?
- from your marriage?

"What do you want?" is the foundational question for all coaching.

There is a second dimension to this question for people of faith. In asking what we want, we are also considering, "What does God want?" When we are at our best, those two considerations stay closely coupled in our discernment process; we weigh both what we want and what God's purpose and creation call for.

In coaching we often begin by posing some version of this substantive question, and then help the person being coached develop a plan to get to the next step. Good coaches help people identify their point A—where they are now—and move toward their point B—where they want to end up.

The question of great substance appears twice in the tenth chapter of Mark. First, Jesus asks the sons of Zebedee, "What do you want from me?" (Mk 10:36 NIV). In this instance, Jesus does not grant them the favored place in heaven they seek. And a few verses later Jesus asks Bartimaeus an almost identical question, "What do you want me to do for you?" (Mk 10:51) This time, because of the man's faith, Jesus restores his sight.

Here are a few other substantial questions Jesus asked:

- "Do you want to get well?" (Jn 5:6)
- "Who do you say I am?" (Mk 8:29)
- "Why were you searching for me?" (Lk 2:49)
- "Why do you call me 'Lord, Lord,' and do not do what I tell you?" (Lk 6:46)
- "Are you listening to me? Really listening?" (Mt 11:15 MSG)

Holy Perception

Jesus had a way of truly seeing people and calling out the best in them. It was almost like he had a sixth sense that allowed him to name demons or know when his robe had been touched, and to home in on the one person in the crowd who needed him the most.

Zacchaeus experienced Jesus' holy perception.

He was trying to see who Jesus was, but on account of the
crowd he could not, because he was short in stature. …
When Jesus came to the place, he looked up and said to
him, "Zacchaeus, hurry and come down; for I must stay
at your house today." (Lk 19:3–5)

In *Jesus: Life Coach*, author Laurie Beth Jones summarizes,

When Jesus encountered the woman at the well her script
was basically: "Fallen woman, living in sin, hiding out
from society." Jesus met her where she was and gave her
a new script: "Bold woman, excited about life, telling all
her friends, supporting a new movement."[1]

Coaches rely on that same holy perception to guide us to those
places of uncommon need and transformation. We trust our intuition to be the deep inner wisdom, guided by the Holy Spirit, that
helps us see what is below the surface and to listen beyond the
words being said. We follow Jesus to those lives and places where
transformation is most needed.

**We follow Jesus to those lives and places where
transformation is most needed.**

Expanding Possibilities

In the eighteenth chapter of Exodus, Moses' father-in-law, Jethro,
comes for a visit and spends the day observing Moses in the role of
a judge settling disputes for people from the whole region.

Obviously, there was no scribe or reporter standing there writing
down what was actually said at the time, but the teller of this story

chose to describe Jethro giving Moses advice and solving his problem for him. Jethro basically told him to deputize other trusted leaders to handle some of the easier cases of dispute, thus leaving the most difficult cases for Moses to decide.

But in your imagination, picture a more coach-like conversation occurring between the two. Can't you picture Jethro observing for a while, and then asking Moses a few coaching questions at the end of an exhausting day. "How is this working out for you?" "What underutilized resources can you enlist?" "Would you like to brainstorm together an alternative approach to this challenge?"

Coaching Is Not Mentoring

One of the clearest biblical examples of the difference between mentoring and coaching is found in the story of young David, who had gotten himself into a situation involving a giant. Out of love, the King tries to help him out.

> Then Saul dressed David in his own tunic. He put a coat of armor on him and a bronze helmet on his head. David fastened on his sword over the tunic and tried walking around, because he was not used to them. "I cannot go in these," he said to Saul, "because I am not used to them." So, he took them off. (1 Sm 17:38–39 NIV)

This is classically what happens when a consultant or mentor attempts to solve another person's challenges by giving advice. Most often the solution being offered does not fit the person with the challenge. This is why we are so deeply committed in coaching to helping individuals do their own work, find their own solutions, answer their own questions, and slay giants their own way.

> **We are deeply committed in coaching to helping individuals do their own work … and slay giants their own way.**

In the end, David finds his own answer to his dilemma. He goes down to the river and picks up five smooth stones, unholsters his sling shot, and puts his trust in God.

A Mature Life

The Apostle Paul invites us to live a mature life in the book of Romans.

> Take your everyday, ordinary life—your sleeping, eating, going-to-work, and walking-around life—and place it before God as an offering. Embracing what God does for you is the best thing you can do for him. Don't become so well adjusted to your culture that you fit into it without even thinking. Instead, fix your attention on God. You'll be changed from the inside out. Readily recognize what he wants from you, and quickly respond to it. Unlike the culture around you, always dragging you down to its level of immaturity, God brings the best out of you, develops well-formed maturity in you. (Rom 12:1–2 MSG)

I believe coaching is a means for a person to take his or her everyday ordinary existence and place it before God. In coaching conversations people dare to crack open their lives, explore facets of who they are, grapple with what they really want and what God really wants of them, and move with determination toward changes that become necessary. It opens the possibility for change from the inside.

Coaching is a means for a person to take his or her every day ordinary existence and place it before God.

Jesus' words reported in Matthew 5:48, "Be you perfect, as your Heavenly Father is perfect," is less of a call to absolute flawless living and more an invitation to live life from a perspective of strong character, maturity, and wholeness. In other words, Jesus invites us to live the mature life we all want, and the life that coaching can help a person discover and take responsibility for living.

Notes

1. Laurie Beth Jones, *Jesus Life Coach* (Nashville, TN, Nelson Business Books, 2004), 24.

3

THE THEOLOGY OF WHOLENESS

Coaches intentionally elect to see others as fundamentally whole. As mentioned in the opening chapter, this is our chosen stance toward those we coach. The relationship begins with *what is right*, rather than *what is wrong*.

My goal as a coach is not to fix a person or to solve his or her problems. The coach's job is to journey and excavate with a client through the layers of what is possible in his or her life and work, steadfastly believing the client has the answers to his or her own questions, and inner wisdom will be the guide to the God-sized things wanting to emerge.

The biblical word translated as "whole" often refers to a person's physical health, as in a person recovering from an illness and feeling well or whole again. But this word is also used as a substitute for "completely," such as,

"And the very God of peace sanctify you wholly; and I pray God your whole spirit and soul and body be preserved blameless unto the coming of our Lord Jesus Christ." (1 Thes 5:23 KJV)

> **Biblical wholeness then goes beyond referencing a physical wellness and implies a complete oneness of being in mind, body, and soul.**

But what does it mean for a Christian coach to consider another person as fundamentally "whole" in light of the reality of brokenness and our sinful nature as taught by the Christian faith? Is the wholeness stance we take in coaching wishful thinking rooted in secular naïveté? Let us look at the concept of wholeness from a variety of theological perspectives.

Made Whole Through Redemption

Paul writes in the third chapter of Romans, verses 23–24, "Since all have sinned and fall short of the glory of God; they are now justified by his grace as a gift, through the redemption that is in Christ Jesus ..." A Calvinist view of theology teaches that one must personally accept Jesus' death on the cross to attain redemption for sin and as the means to their salvation. This perspective maintains we are people of total depravity, and some are "elected" to be saved while others are condemned to damnation.

What then makes a person whole from this perspective?

A coach with that theology maintains that wholeness refers to the state of restoration to God because God has redeemed or saved that person. Jesus' death and resurrection have restored the individual from a state of sinfulness to wholeness with God. That person is now in right relationship with the Creator.

In other words, according to this view the client is not *naturally whole*, but rather is *made whole* in Jesus through redemption.

> According to this view the client is not *naturally whole*, but rather is *made whole* in Jesus through redemption.

This perspective may make sense to many within the context of Christianity, but where does that leave the coach or the client who is of another faith or who is completely averse to religion? Are those individuals then fundamentally not whole?

In God's Image

Let's consider another way of looking at wholeness. *Imago Dei* is a Latin phrase used theologically in Judaism, Christianity, and Sufi Islam to assert that human beings are created in the image of God, as conveyed in Genesis 1:27.

RUMINATION

Dr. Drew Dyson, trained coach, district superintendent of the Raritan Valley District in the Greater New Jersey Conference of the United Methodist Church, former professor of practical theology at Wesley Theological Seminary, Washington, DC

> *From the perspective of Wesleyan theology, a theology of wholeness is rooted in the doctrine of prevenient grace. This begins with the assertion that all people are created in the imago Dei. Being created in the image of God means that humans held the capacity for the full love of God and of humanity. In a relational way of being rooted in Eastern traditions, the essence of the imago Dei is the capacity for wholeness in relationship with God, with oneself, and with others.*

In his sermon "On the Fall of Man," Wesley contends that the result of the fall of humanity is the partial loss of the imago Dei and a loss of a primary relationship with God, thereby distorting our human relationships (with self and others) as well. Humans, whose relationship with God was broken, lost the capacity for the fullness of love for God and humanity. Further, the ability to understand the works of God and to have one's affections turned toward God became distorted.

Wesley's doctrine of prevenient grace, put forth in his sermon "The New Birth," contends that because of God's divine action in Jesus Christ and through the presence of the Holy Spirit, "no human was wholly void of the grace of God." Every human being bears both the mark of original sin and the imprint of God's nature through God's grace. In this way, Wesley forcefully argues that despite the brokenness we all experience, through the work of God's grace, there is an undeniable element of the imago Dei present in all human beings—whether it is claimed and recognized as such or not.

In light of this affirmation, one is left to wonder whether the role of the coach is to journey alongside another human being, using the tools and strategies of effective coaching to help the client uncover and claim the integrated wholeness which lies at the heart of their identity as one created in the image of God.

Being created in God's likeness implies a wholeness not earned or obtained through redemption but rather imprinted on the soul from the very beginning. It is an original blessing. Each child is born with it. A coach might say the people they coach are whole because that is their original state of being.

> Being created in God's likeness implies a wholeness ...
> imprinted on the soul from the very beginning.

Christian theologian Fred Craddock reminds us that in the book of Genesis the creation comes before the fall, not the other way around. God, who created humankind in the likeness and image of God, at the very outset pronounced that creation "Good!"

Christian coaches may faithfully choose to believe that the people they coach are naturally creative, resourceful, and whole. This is true whether the person being coached is a Christian, Muslim, Buddhist, or agnostic. Wholeness is not related to Jesus, but to the natural state of being as part of God's good creation.

Quaker theologian Parker Palmer writes, "We are cursed with the blessing of consciousness and choice, a two-edged sword that both divides us and can help us become whole. ...The divided life may be endemic, but wholeness is always a choice."[1] He continues, "Wholeness does not mean perfection: it means embracing broken-ness as an integral part of life. Knowing this gives me hope that human wholeness—mine, yours, ours—need not be a utopian dream, if we can use devastation as a seedbed for new life."[2]

> "Wholeness does not mean perfection: it means embracing brokenness as an integral part of life."
>
> —PARKER PALMER

What we mean by original wholeness can also be considered from the lens of the Jewish understanding of *shalom*. This Hebrew noun refers to the oneness, prosperity, and peace of God's creation.

Shalom is the state of perfect harmony that God built into the design of the world from the very beginning, and it is still God's perfect vision for creation, even though we seem to have a difficult time realizing that vision. It is akin to the view of perfection preached by John Wesley, the founder of the Methodist movement. According to Wesley, perfection was our original state and remains a compelling goal on the horizon toward which all Christian living should be heading.

Coaches know that wholeness is not the perpetual state for the people we coach, because we know all too well the tendencies toward temptation and sinful separation—starting with our own lives. Oneness with God is a beginning state, but not a permanent state.

Grace, then, is the gift of realizing that God has decided to love us anyway, even in our state of separation and sinfulness. We are not loved because we are good; we are loved because God is good.

> For I am convinced that neither death, nor life, nor angels,
> nor rulers, nor things present, nor things to come, nor
> powers, nor height, nor depth, nor anything else in all
> creation, will be able to separate us from the love of God
> in Christ Jesus our Lord. (Rom 8:39)

The Coach's Stance Is Wholeness

Some Christian coaches see a client as made whole or restored to wholeness through Jesus' redemptive actions. Others see a client as naturally whole because they are *Imago Dei*, or they see that person as God first saw them, even though the person's actions may at times separate them from their primal wholeness.

To take the position that a person is "whole" is not an individually determined character judgment or an evaluative statement of his or her human condition, as though some people are whole and others are not. It is the theological declaration of a truth about someone's essential substance, and a truth that is reflected in all created life.

Regardless of how we get there theologically, the coach's stance is wholeness, and our end game is participating with God and the client in the transformation of life. We begin our coaching work from here!

Regardless of how we get there theologically ... our end game is participating with God and the client in the transformation of life.

Notes

1. Parker Palmer, *A Hidden Wholeness: The Journey Toward an Undivided Life* (San Francisco, CA: Jossey-Bass, 2009), 5.
2. Parker Palmer, *A Hidden Wholeness: The Journey Toward an Undivided Life* (San Francisco, CA: Jossey-Bass, 2009), 17.

PART II

ON FINDING AND BECOMING A COACH

4

WHAT TO LOOK FOR WHEN CHOOSING A COACH

Once you decide you are ready to work with a coach, where do you begin the process of selection?

The internet is flooded with people offering coaching services, so narrowing the field and deciding on the coach who will best match your needs can be an arduous process.

A Coach Does Not Need to Be an Expert in a Specific Area of Need

A key principle to consider in meeting the task of finding the right coach is that a good coach can coach a bishop, a pilot, and a rodeo clown with the same level of effectiveness. While there are coaches specializing in church planting or in congregational revitalization or in leadership development, the search for a coach should not be limited to coaches within a specific area of concentration. The power is not in the coach's occupation-specific expertise. It is in the coach's ability to help unleash the expertise, passion, and potential of the person being coached.

> A good coach can coach a bishop, a pilot, and a rodeo clown with the same level of effectiveness.

Following are eight recommendations for finding the right coach.

1. Seek a credentialed coach. Perhaps the most important selection criteria is seeking someone who is credentialed by the International Coach Federation (ICF). If you would only employ a doctor who is a member of the American Medical Association, doesn't it make sense to require the same level of professional vetting for a coach? The initials listed behind the coach's signature indicates his or her level of training.

The ICF offers three levels of coaching credentials:

a. Associate Certified Coach (ACC) is a newer coach with at least 100 hours of coaching experience.

b. Professional Certified Coach (PCC) is a more advanced coach with additional training and over 500 hours of coaching experience.

c. Master Certified Coach (MCC) is the highest level of coach with over 2500 hours of coaching experience.

The International Coach Federation is the standard-bearer for proficiency in the field of coaching, assuring that the credentialed coach has an appropriate amount of training, mentoring, and coaching experience. This coach will also be bound to an important code of ethical conduct and professional practice. An extensive list of credentialed coaches can be found on the ICF website.

> The ICF is the standard-bearer for proficiency in the field of coaching.

2. Avoid "spiritual coaches." Some coaches working in the field of ministry advertise themselves as *spiritual coaches*. However, an internet search for that term reveals that most are untrained, not credentialed, and fall more into the category of New Age guidance. One spiritual coach provides a lecture series on avoiding "The Dark Side"; another will channel messages from beyond the grave through her cat, and still others will gladly share their wisdom and advice using a formula for success they have created. Honestly, it gets pretty weird in the field of "spiritual coaching."

Most coaches working in the field of ministry refer to themselves as a leadership coach, discipleship coach, transformation coach, clergy coach, ministry coach, faith coach, or congregational coach.

3. Interview several coaches. Choosing a coach can take time; allow time for discernment. It is standard practice in the field of coaching to interview several potential coaches as part of the decision-making process, so it is not necessary to hide the fact that you are interviewing several coaches at the same time.

Before you interview potential coaches in person or on the phone, discover as much as possible about them from personal references or internet resources. Read about their strengths, areas of expertise, and their level of training. For example, the Holmes Coaching Group lists a number of qualified affiliate coaches, each with his or her picture, biography, and level of training. www.holmescoaching.com.

Once you've selected a coach, the courteous best practice is to inform the other coaches you have interviewed about the decision you have made.

4. Don't underestimate the power of phone and video coaching. Face-to-face communication that allows the ability to perceive physical reactions and body language has clear benefits. However, for practical reasons a great deal of coaching takes place over the phone or via Skype, Facetime, or some other video interface. Phone and video coaching have proven to be highly effective and are even preferred by some clients. Coaches are trained to compensate for distance by being highly present on the phone, and by listening at very deep levels to what is being said, what is happening in the spaces, and what is not being said.

However, deciding what medium to use for the coaching interaction should ultimately be left to the client. If being coached in person is important to you, then select a coach willing to accommodate that desire.

5. Do a chemistry test. Strong emotional chemistry is essential to a productive coaching relationship. Trust is absolutely essential. It is worth asking yourself these questions in hiring a coach.

- "Do I feel like I can talk freely with this coach about any aspect of my life?
- "Is this someone I would look forward to having a regular extended conversation with about the things that matter most to me?"
- "Is this person listening to me, more that talking to me?"

Often there is a palpable spiritual resonance to the chemistry between a coach and a client. If the client becomes uncomfortable in interaction with the coach at any time, that concern should be raised for discussion, and if the concern cannot be resolved, it is time to find a new coach.

6. Inquire about "free samples." Most coaches offer a free initial coaching session lasting anywhere from twenty to fifty minutes. During that time, the coach should be able to answer all of your questions about coaching and also demonstrate some of his or her basic proficiency in coaching. Taking advantage of this offer not only gives you the benefit of a free coaching session, but also the opportunity to gain a feel for the coach's style and approach prior to committing. Some coaches may also use this sample session to determine their own compatibility with you.

7. Expect to pay for quality in coaching. In 2012, the average hourly rate for a leadership/executive coach was $229.[1] Coaching is regarded as an extremely valuable resource in the corporate world and increasingly so within religious circles, and high-quality coaching is generally well compensated. However, many adequately trained, ICF-certified Christian coaches charge between $100 and $150 per hour or offer a sliding scale in an intentional effort to be more affordable for nonprofit organizations and leaders. For example, one of the core values of the Holmes Coaching Group is affordability, along with excellence and diversity.

Coaching is regarded as an extremely valuable resource in the corporate world and increasingly so within religious circles.

Some coaches offer group coaching as a more economical option. An even more cost-effective alternative is to hire a coach who is in the process of being trained as a coach. These students will sometimes request permission to audio record the coaching session so it can be played back for assessment by a professional mentor coach as part of the coach's learning.

8. Sign a coaching covenant. The International Coaching Federation requires that coaching which is being provided as a fee for service be accompanied by a written agreement. This agreement is also sometimes referred to as a *designed alliance, contract,* or *covenant.* This agreement covers the expectations the coach and client have for working together. It clarifies details such as scheduling, compensation, frequency of calls, confidentiality, number of sessions, fee for missed sessions, and contact information. The coaching covenant we use for the Holmes Coaching Group also asks for the client to respond to some initial coaching questions, such as "What are three goals you would like to work on in our time together?" "What challenges keep you awake at night?" and "What else would you like for me to know about you so that I can best coach you?"

Coaching Is an Investment in Becoming Your Best Self

God intends for your life to be fully lived and beckons you to be your best in work, play, faith, and personal relationships. Hiring a trained Christian coach is an investment in the immensely fabulous and astounding *you*!

5

TRAINING TO BECOME A COACH

The journey to becoming a coach is one of mastering new competencies and of learning about one's self. Actually, most coaching skills are not entirely new. They are proficiencies most people already possess, but coach training teaches them to use the skills in conjunction with one another as a muscle group.

Five Major Coaching Skills

These five major skills work together to form the basic muscle group in coaching.

1. Presence. We have all experienced the power of being intently listened to by another person who is completely present to us. We feel understood and known when we are listened to with such intention. Coaching requires the coach's undivided attention giving complete focus to the client.

2. Deep Listening. Psychologist David Augsberger writes, "Being heard is so close to being loved that for the average person, they are almost indistinguishable."[1]

In a coach-approach conversation, we strive to listen at the deepest level possible. This means we listen for the client's inflections and emotions. We listen to where the energy is in the person, to what choices are being made, to where the resistance is, to what is happening in the silences and even what is not being said.

"**Being heard is so close to being loved that for the average person, they are almost indistinguishable.**"

—DAVID AUGSBERGER

The listening we do in coaching is not just remaining silent or passive. It is not just parroting back or reflectively listening. We actually maximize the communication by participating in the conversation, calling the client forth, and voicing what we are noticing from that place of deep listening.

3. Powerful Questions. A coaching conversation is driven forward by the questions asked by the coach, and occasionally the coach is able to land an especially powerful question. These questions are usually short and open-ended, and stop the person being coached in his or her tracks. They get the person to dig deeper and grow further. If the coaching conversation were an automobile in motion, then powerful questions would be the engine.

If the coaching conversation were an automobile in motion, then powerful questions would be the engine.

4. Expanding Possibilities. Often in our lives, we come up with an idea that may even be a great idea, but we settle too soon with that one idea before taking the time to explore a whole range of related possibilities. We also tend to limit what is possible by what we believe to be true based on narrow assumptions; for example, "I don't have the money now; I am not that important; I am too busy."

The coach's job is to help the person being coached identify a primary held perspective, and then challenge him or her to envision other possible perspectives. We raise questions prompting a variety of other ways of looking at the situation.

5. Action Planning with Accountability. The key objective of the coach-approach conversation is to help individuals move from where they are to where they want to be. This implies that they want to take action to attain their goals. Our conversations move people from a wish or a hope to an action plan with some built-in accountability.

Core Competencies of Coaching

The International Coach Federation actually lists eleven core competencies of coaching, which every coach must learn and adequately demonstrate. They are:

1. Meeting Ethical Guidelines and Professional Standards

2. Establishing the Coaching Agreement

3. Establishing Trust and Intimacy with the Client

4. Coaching Presence

5. Active Listening

6. Powerful Questioning

7. Direct Communication

8. Creating Awareness

9. Designing Actions

10. Planning and Goal Setting

11. Managing Progress and Accountability

Excellence Is a Requirement

There is no place in Christian coaching for coaching lite. Those who would coach clergy leaders and laity in the church need to be the most highly trained coaches available who manifest excellence in the work they do. It is not only what clergy and laity deserve and the church needs, but it is what God expects.

There is no place in Christian coaching for coaching lite.

The most extensive research ever conducted on the profession of coaching reveals that the leading obstacle for this vocation is the myriad of people who self-identify as a "coach" but who are not actually trained or credentialed as a coach.[2] Fortunately, since 2013 most clergy and denominational leaders are only hiring credentialed coaches who are trained and who adequately represent the modality and profession of coaching.

RUMINATION

Wanda Duckett, trained coach, district superintendent of the Baltimore Metropolitan District of the Baltimore-Washington Conference of the United Methodist Church

I would not go to a coach who was not ICF credentialed. As with anything, I think people need to be trained and equipped to do their jobs well, but especially coaches who have the potential to be so helpful, or to be so hurtful if they are not trained. Coaching is art and science, and the training helps hone both of those areas.

I use coaching not only in pastoring and superintending, but I use it in parenting, with friends, and even with prayer partners who may be working through something. It is a good life skill that I utilize in many of my interactions. Coaching is now a part of who I am.

Four Steps to Becoming an ICF Credentialed Coach

Think of coaching as a four-step process. Each phase has been intentionally established by the International Coach Federation. The most current information about this process can be found on the ICF website at https://coachfederation.org.

- Step One is selecting and completing an ICF accredited 60 to 120-hour coach training program. Advice about what questions to ask and how to determine an appropriate training program is provided in the next section of this chapter.
- Step Two is choosing a mentor coach to provide ten hours of mentor coaching. This mentor coach will coach you on your coaching of others, offering verbal and written assessments of how well you utilize the eleven core competencies of coaching.
- Step Three is providing 100 hours of coaching to others after your coach training has commenced. During this "practice period," you are working toward proficiency in the art and practice of coaching.
- Step Four is providing proof of completion of the first three steps along with an application for credentialing as an associate certified coach with the ICF. This requires

adherence to the ICF Code of Ethics and successful completion of the Coach Knowledge Assessment, a written multiple-choice test administered by the ICF. Learn more at https://coachfederation.org/code-of-ethics/.

Note: It is possible for the first three steps to overlap and even take place concurrently.

Coach Training Landscape

The International Coach Federation does not itself provide coach-specific training, but to ensure quality training it does accredit coach training programs that meet its high standards. As the accrediting body, the ICF cannot recommend any particular training programs.

There are hundreds of accredited programs listed on the ICF website. These are divided into categories such as career and transition, health and wellness, leadership, spirituality, small business, and others. Options abound if the training you seek is to be provided by a secular coach training program. Two of the largest and most well-known are Coach Training Institute (CTI), http://www.coactive.com/ and Coach U http://www.coachu-hq.com/; both hold in-person trainings all over the world and even offer some online courses. A few universities now offer coach training as well.

Choices are more limited when it comes to all ICF-accredited training programs geared especially for use in ministry. The curriculum for all ICF-accredited programs is tied directly to the eleven core competencies of coaching, but what is unique about these programs is their application in the realm of ministry; our Coach Approach Skills Training is in this category. The strength and reputation of each of these programs does vary, so it is important to solicit recommendations from trusted sources.

Choices are more limited when it comes to ICF accredited training programs geared especially for use in ministry.

Here are some good questions to consider in selecting a program:

How much will the training cost? The range of financial investment for being trained is remarkable. Secular coach training schools typically charge more and offer established locations and regular schedules for training.

Training programs specifically geared for ministry are more favorably priced. The program I helped develop and now teach has been extensively utilized by major denominations, in part because the cost for the training is considerably less than other training programs. We are introducing the power of the coach approach to ministry as far and wide as possible in all Christian denominations, which also means keeping it affordable.

More information about the Coach Approach Skills Training (CAST) Fast Track is available at the end of this book or online at www.holmescoaching.com.

We are introducing the power of the coach approach to ministry as far and wide as possible in all Christian denominations.

How long will the training take? The number of months devoted to training varies according to each program and can be governed by the pace at which a student wants to proceed. A part-time pastor or retiree might choose to progress through the training at a different rate than a full-time pastor might choose.

The minimum requirement for coach-specific accredited training is sixty hours. Some programs offer up to 120 hours or more, which obviously takes a longer period of time along with greater financial commitment.

A few training programs offer courses over a concentrated period of time for participants who elect a deep dive into training. Our sixty-hour FAST TRACK training requires one month of pre-work, one week of in-person onsite training offered at various locations around the country, and eight weeks of video-based webinars. Students complete the required sixty hours over a four-month period. Once we began offering this option, it quickly became our most sought-after training.

Is in-person or online training preferred? Certain coaching programs only offer in-person training, others present a virtual platform for training, and still others tender an option of either or a combination of both.

Deciding on the best delivery method should not be solely based on convenience and affordability but should also take into account the value conveyed by the method of teaching. In the highly relational work of coaching, the experience of spending a week or more with classmates learning in-person from a team of live instructors is significantly different from a virtual learning experience.

The training is not the only cost involved in becoming a credentialed coach. There are additional costs associated with the other phases of the coaching process.

Here is a breakdown of the total investment in becoming a coach:

ICF Accredited Coach Specific Training $1,900–$15,000

10 Hours of Mentor Coaching $1,200–$1,800

100 Hours Coaching Clients $0

ICF Application and Test $100–$600

Many training programs provide options to pay up front or on a schedule over time.

Ethics and Continuing Education

With the formation of the International Coach Federation in 1995 came not only professional standards and training criterion for those who hold themselves out to be coaches, but also the development of a recognized Code of Ethics.[3] Additionally, the ICF enforces standards for ongoing continuing education to maintain certification. For coaches, these advances are especially important for legitimizing the field, and the Code of Ethics gives the ICF a mechanism through which to regulate a professional standard of behavior in coaching.

The ICF Code of Ethics is substantively similar to the professional ethics employed by the fields of counseling, social work, and ministry. It is comprehensive in addressing not only a coach's interaction with a client, but also in handling situations like third-party payments and issues of privacy and confidentiality. It requires adherence to the acceptable standards for research when publishing in the field of coaching and an accurate representation of the coach's experience and level of training, and encourages referral to professionals in other helping modalities when appropriate.

The ICF does maintain an ethics review board to hear ethical complaints formally lodged with the organization. And a coach's credential can be removed for violation of the ICF's Code of Ethics.

A Word of Caution

A quick internet search will reveal numerous Christian coach training programs being marketed online that are not associated with or accredited by the International Coach Federation. Buyer beware!

The certification these trainings offer is a certificate of completion in their particular program that holds little value or credibility in the wider field of coaching. Their websites and printed material may look impressive, their specialty certificates enticing, and their accreditation authentic. But look closely: the accrediting body is sometimes of their own creation with initials close to the ICF, like the "ICE" or "IFC."

I have spoken with more than one leader of a non-accredited program who holds the position that a Christian coach training program is spiritual work, which does not need approval of some secular body like the ICF. Meeting the high standards of ICF accreditation with another program is doubtful because they substitute a subtle agenda of conversion of the client to the Christian faith for the foundational principle of client-centered coaching. There may be other reasons as well that certain programs decide not to be accredited.

The following profiles of a coach and client are highlights from a survey of over 15,000 coaches from 137 countries from the 2016 ICF Global Coaching Study.[4]

Profile of a Coach

The average coach is either European (35 percent) or North American (33 percent) and is a trained and professionally credentialed coach.

In North America, three out of four coaches are female.

The estimated global total revenue from coaching in 2015 was $2.3 billion, which is a 19 percent increase over the 2011 estimate.

The average coach makes $61,900 per year from coaching.

Most coaches combine coaching with another professional skill such as consulting, teaching, or counseling.

A huge majority of coaches feel strongly that coaching is able to influence social change. This is especially true of coaches in Latin America, the Caribbean, the Middle East and Africa.

Profile of a Client

An average coaching client is under the age of forty-five.

The typical client works as a manager (29 percent) or an executive (23 percent).

Only 19 percent of people being coached pay for it personally. Most coaching is paid for by an organization.

Seventy-eight percent of the clients who hire a coach expect their coach to be credentialed. In the survey, trained coaches reported the number one obstacle in the coaching profession is untrained individuals calling themselves a coach (44 percent) and the confusion that creates about coaching (35 percent).

Notes

1. "David W. Augsberger—Quotable Quote—Quotes," Quotes, Goodreads, last accessed March 18, 2018, https://www.goodreads.com/quotes/288161-being-heard-is-so-close-to-being-loved-that-for.

2. "2012 ICF Global Coaching Study," Executive Summary, International Coach Federation, last modified 2017, https://coachfederation.org/app/uploads/2017/12/2012I CFGlobalCoachingStudy-ExecutiveSummary.pdf.

3. "Code of Ethics," ICF Code of Ethics, International Coach Federation. last accessed March 21, 2018, https://coachfederation.org/code-of-ethics/.

4. "2016 ICF Global Coaching Study," Executive Summary, International Coach Federation, last accessed March 27, 2018, https://coachfederation.org/app/uploads/2017/12/2016I CFGlobalCoachingStudy_ExecutiveSummary-2.pdf.

6

NUTS AND BOLTS OF LIFE AS A COACH

Some trained coaches never establish a coaching practice with actual coaching clients; instead they adopt the "coach approach" to ministry as a style of leadership by integrating the skills they have learned into all aspects of their life and ministry. In Chapter 7 we will examine more specifically what that general application to ministry looks like.

People who work full-time in the field of coaching fall into two categories: they are either internal coaches or independent coaches.

In the corporate setting, coaches who are part of a system and also trained to coach within that system are referred to as "internal coaches." Many of the coaches with whom I associate are internal coaches for NASA, county governments, and large for-profit organizations. There are also large coaching firms that hire coaches as contractors. The nature of this coaching is sometimes distinct from life coaching and is far more goal oriented. What I hear from my internal-coaching friends is that they feel their coaching is sometimes restrained and too narrowly focused on outcomes or performance improvement.

In the world of churches, most internal coaching is provided as one aspect of the work of a supervisor or provided by a peer who has been trained as a coach.

This chapter is an overview of pros and cons of independent coaching and the best practices for those who want to formally launch a coaching practice and offer their service to clients.

Independent Coaching: Pros and Cons

Before you decide to become a coach, you might find it helpful to consider some of the advantages and disadvantages of the profession.

Advantages of Independent Coaching

In addition to the feeling of independence that comes when working for oneself, the personal and financial rewards can also be enticing. Here are some other advantages.

Tremendous Impact. By far the greatest benefit of being a coach is the satisfaction that comes in making a significant difference in another person's life. Coaching is the most direct and effective means to life and organizational transformation. Of course, we know that God is a major part of this process, which means the results are often truly stunning. Independent coaches have the autonomy to organize their coaching practice for maximum impact on the lives of people they coach.

Coaching is the most direct and effective means to life and organizational transformation.

Life-Giving Work. People who struggle with low performance issues usually do not seek out the help of a coach, and people working on their pain or feelings of brokenness turn to counselors or other health professionals. This means that the people generally drawn to coaching are relatively healthy, motivated, and eager about the possibilities for their life. This work is energizing rather than draining, which is why many counselors and other mental health professionals have actually left their professions to be trained as coaches. Often at the end of a day of coaching clients, I feel fully alive and content.

> **The people generally drawn to coaching are relatively healthy, motivated, and eager about the possibilities for their life.**

Coaches Are Enjoyable. Coaches tend to be some of the most vibrant, creative, and highly relational people you will meet. In short, they are a fun group of people to hang out with, learn from, and collaborate with.

Working from Home. Coaching is often done over the phone, which means a coach can literally work from any location that has strong phone or internet service. I've met coaches who choose to live in Bali and Fiji and just navigate the time zones to meet with clients who are from all over the world. Setting up a home office in a spare room in your house can be a lot more cost-effective than renting office space.

Flexible Scheduling. Because coaches manage their own weekly calendar, it is possible to build coaching availability around the rhythms of family life or another part-time job. Coaching availability can also expand or contract depending on the size of the client load.

Low Overhead Cost. With a relatively small investment in a computer, a good phone and headset, some business cards, and a website, a coach can launch as a small business working from home without incurring major expense. The largest outlay most coaches make is the cost of their coach training. As a coaching practice grows, expenses such as administrative assistance, travel, and the help of an accountant are often added.

A coach can launch as a small business working from home without incurring major expense.

Wage Determination. The coach establishes his or her hourly rates for coaching and daily rates for presentations or teaching; these are often influenced by the industry standards. Because those decisions do not require approval from other stakeholders, they can be flexible, and rates can be adjusted higher or lower as needed. Many coaches have a tiered rate structure ranging from basic coaching services to more comprehensive packages of availability.

Limited Liability. Most coaches do not carry liability insurance because their exposure to the kinds of things for which they would need coverage is minimal. Therapeutic work done by mental health professionals requires insurance coverage because they deal with specific diagnoses and are open to issues like transference. These issues are much less prevalent in coaching. However, coaching insurance is offered through the ICF for a very nominal fee for those coaches who want it.

Continual Growth. The ICF coaching credential must be renewed every three years by accruing a certain number of continuing education units. Opportunities to earn these credits are offered in-person at global gatherings in interesting places in the world and at local ICF chapter meetings, and they are also offered online. Coaches tend to be committed, life-long learners.

Cons of Independent Coaching

The life of an independent coach isn't all roses. Here are some issues to consider.

Isolation. The concern I hear voiced most often from independent coaches is how alone they can feel. Our work is having coaching conversations with clients, but for many coaches those conversations are not a suitable replacement for the experience of working in an active office environment with co-workers. If you are a "people person," which most coaches are, seclusion can be especially problematic.

Working from Home. While maintaining a home office may have its advantages in terms of convenience and cost, it can also prove to be a disadvantage. People working from home sometimes struggle to maintain clear boundaries between work and home life. During off hours, work is always in the next room. During working hours, the laundry is always just down the hall. Working from home may also complicate issues of security and privacy for seeing clients in person.

Financial Vulnerability. With a steady paycheck comes a certain peace of mind, even when the job itself may not be gratifying. Independent coaches have often traded one for the other. Coaches face a prevalent sense of dis-ease tied to not knowing where their next contract will come from. It is the underlying angst shared by many self-employed people.

Coaches face a prevalent sense of dis-ease tied to not knowing where their next contract will come from.

Limited Health Benefits. Self-employment comes with no built-in package of retirement or health benefits. Adequate arrangements must be made for coverage in other ways. Private health insurance may be so expensive that it is prohibitive.

As you can see, there are many factors to weigh in envisioning the future as a coach. The decision about what would be best for one person will differ from what makes the most sense for another.

Best Practice for Establishing a Coaching Practice

After considering all the pros and cons, if you still want to be a coach you will want to pay attention to the following best practices compiled by the Holmes Coaching Group.

Develop a Purpose Statement. Clarity about who you are as a coach and what you are offering the world is essential. Development of a well-honed purpose statement, or what some call an *elevator speech*, not only increases your own lucidity about your function as a coach but also helps others promptly discern what you are offering to them.

The worst thing you can do when telling another person about your coaching is give a halting and muddled explanation. Your statement should be concise, crystalize what you offer as a coach, and be memorizable so it is ready at a moment's notice. Communicate confident precision, not uncertainty.

Communicate confident precision, not uncertainty.

This purpose statement I heard from a coach a few years ago is still memorable: "I walk with leaders to the dangerous edge of what is possible and help them take a flying leap." Doesn't that make you just want to get out your checkbook, write a big check, and get started with that coach?

Don't Play Small. If you are truly convinced that coaching is God's work, it is worth doing prodigiously and with colossal results in mind.

I will never forget the night in a hotel room with my coach-trainer partner, George Howard, when we dared to articulate out loud for the first time the outcome we presumed we would attain through our coach-training efforts. We decided we would not stop short of "reshaping the way leadership happens in all Christian denominations."

I am sure there is a slender line between inspired faithfulness and audacious conceit, but I can tell you that after being doggedly committed to this work for nine years, there is growing evidence of progress toward our colossal presumption.

Recognize that You Are Starting a Business.

As a new full-time coach, I thought I was starting a coaching ministry, but I was wrong. In reality, I was becoming a small business owner first. My "product" just happens to be coaching rather than replacement windows.

The vast majority of us who are in ministry have no experience in marketing, sending invoices, budgeting for fixed and soft costs, monetizing our time, and a myriad of details associated with being a small business owner. Our education was in the humanities, not in economics. Yet to be a successful coach, one needs to have a certain business acumen, or at least the ability to partner with someone who does.

In the process of establishing a coaching practice, I discovered I had a previously unidentified aptitude for writing proposals, crunching numbers, and projecting revenue. Who knew? As you launch into the field of coaching, be prepared to grow and be stretched in areas that may not be your existing expertise.

To be a successful coach, one needs to have a certain business acumen.

You will also want to develop a system for staying organized concerning coaching notes, contracts, invoices, and payments. If organization is not one of your strengths, find help from someone who has that gift. My life shifted dramatically the day my business grew to the point I could hire a virtual assistant, and everything about my work became structured and professional.

Cluster Your Availability. Going from a meeting to a coaching session, then to a counseling session, and then back again to coaching is not likely to result in a coach's best work. Where possible, organize your calendar by clustering your availability for coaching into blocks of time. For instance, maybe you coach Tuesdays from 9:00 a.m. to 1:00 p.m. and again Thursday afternoons and evenings.

Standard routine in the field of coaching is to offer a fifty-minute coaching session once or twice per month to each client. Blocking out periods of availability for coaching also creates space during the week for other important aspects of growing a coaching practice.

Make Time for Marketing. Church leaders are not typically wired for self-promotion, but successful coaches find a way to foster attention. My one friend (who ironically is a vegetarian) says, "Now that I only eat what I kill, I am much more intentional about the hunt."

Every hour a coach spends coaching a client is the consequence of two hours of marketing, networking, and connecting. In fact, some experts would tell you that being a good coach is not enough. What matters even more is how connected and trusted you are in an arena where your coaching might be of benefit.

> **Every hour a coach spends coaching a client is the consequence of two hours of marketing, networking, and connecting.**

I realize my own transition to full-time coaching is not that helpful as an example to others, due to a number of uniquely favorable factors. I transitioned from being an internal coach in my conference to being an independent coach with budding national recognition and close affiliation with influential leaders in my denomination. That exceptional good fortune removed much of the suffering in my transition to full-time independent coaching, for which I am profoundly grateful.

Obviously, the most fruitful way to market oneself as a coach is not through cold calling, but by naturally maximizing connections you already have to genuinely offer coaching to those who already know and respect you.

Marketing your coaching skills can be done with integrity. It has never once made me feel slimy or disingenuous. And what helps the most is to remember that this is substantially not about you. It is about God. It is about offering what God is able to do in the lives of others through your coaching.

> **Remember that this is substantially not about you. It is about God.**

Develop a Compelling Presentation. Have you ever attended a workshop or presentation and left thinking, *I would give just about anything to get to spend more time with that presenter*? You want to be that presenter.

Consider developing an interesting seminar, speech, or presentation that has universal appeal to a wide number of people. Choose something in which you have expertise or experience, or a powerful story. You have something to offer than no one else does; find what that thing is. Make it compelling, get really good a presenting it, and take it on the road.

You have something to offer than no one else does: find what that thing is.

Obviously, this will also require promoting or marketing what you have to offer.

In the last five minutes of your presentation, say, "I happen to be a professional coach, and up front here is a sign-up sheet. If you would like to talk with me further about this or receive some help implementing these strategies when you get home, please sign up. The first session is free."

A business coach I once worked with assures me that the math around what happens next is predictable. If there are twenty people in the room, six will sign up for an initial free session. Of those six, four or five of them will commit to ongoing coaching with you.

Combine Your Coaching. The 2016 ICF Global Coaching Study, undertaken by PricewaterhouseCoopers, indicates that very few people coach exclusively as a vocation. Those who strictly coach consider themselves to be employed part-time and earning supplemental income.

Very few people coach exclusively as a vocation.

Most coaches wind up combining coaching with an additional helping discipline such as consulting, teaching, or counseling. Some meld three or more of these disciplines together.

It would be wise for you to consider what else you might offer the world to augment the coaching you provide.

Stay Connected. There is great opportunity in coaching to continue to grow as a coach and collaborate with other coaches. Yet independent coaches often feel isolated from their coaching peers as they manage their own practice and work primarily from a home office. Almost every major metropolitan area possesses a local chapter of the International Coach Federation. Even if you are located in a rural area away from a major city, it is occasionally worth traveling to local chapter meetings for the purpose of staying connected to other coaches.

You might even consider helping to form a local chapter of the ICF if one does not exist in your area. I participated in that effort as a founding member of the Maryland chapter of the ICF and served two years as president of the chapter. The association with other coaches in the field has added immeasurable value to my work.

You will also want to maintain relationships with the people you met when you were being trained as a coach. In many cases, those individuals turn out to be the core of your ongoing supportive coaching community.

Pray As You Go. Every coach has experienced what it is like to begin a coaching conversation unprepared. We try our best not to let it show, but the individuals we are coaching instinctively pick up on it. They can tell right away if we are divinely poised for God to do something amazing in the conversation or if we are feeling discombobulated.

Without question, the most important five minutes of any coaching session are the five minutes prior to the client arriving in person or picking up the phone. This critical time allows the coach to clear away distractions, like silencing a secondary phone, turning off the computer screen, or closing the door to the room. It also allows for getting mentally and spiritually ready.

The most important five minutes of any coaching session is the five minutes prior to the client arriving.

In those few minutes, pray that God will use you in just the right way to be a wide-open channel of God's work. Ask God to get you out of the way so that you can be the best coach you can be in service to the coaching relationship.

RUMINATION

Rev. Dr. Rodney Smothers, trained coach, Director of Leadership and Congregational Development for the Baltimore-Washington Conference of the United Methodist Church

During the coaching experience, prayer is that divine accompaniment which shows up as a welcomed guest, connecting both the coach and the coachee in a way that words alone cannot do. Prayer serves many times as an anchor in the coaching experience. While not intended to be advice, prayer can bring up a response to questions that have not yet been thought of but often reveal themselves in the impartation of wisdom and knowledge that arise in the act of prayer.

In my experience, clergy are particularly receptive to prayer as a part of the coaching process because it affirms that the coach is also aware of the movement of the Holy Spirit in the midst of the coaching conversations.

Prayer is a nonthreatening vehicle which invites self-discovery and spiritual anchoring and is an additional resource for clarification of potential insight gained during the coaching encounter.

Prayer is a chance to remind the coach and the client together that they are in the presence of the Holy and that it would be well to listen for the Divine Word revealed in the midst of their human words. This is an opportunity for the coaching relationship to become incarnate in the Spirit of Christ.

Get a Coach. Most coaches have a coach. If coaching is a helping modality you believe in, invest in it yourself.

Over the years I have paid many different coaches to coach me, and in the process, I experientially learned more about coaching from every one of them. An affordable alternative is to partner with another coach to reciprocate in coaching one another, as a barter rather than for compensation.

PART III

CLERGY COACHING
APPLICATIONS

7

THE COACH-APPROACH PASTOR

The majority of clergy who have been trained in coaching use coaching skills as a natural form of leadership for ministry in the local church. Let's see what that might look like and how it differs from a more conventional style of clergy leadership.

A well-developed traditional style of clergy leadership is the directive approach. The pastor is the "go-to" answer person. The pastor chooses the discipleship curriculum, decides the theme for the stewardship campaign, and even selects the color for the new chairs in the meeting room. Small and even medium-size churches often expect this style of leadership from their pastors.

Coach-approach pastors tend to listen more and advise less in their work with church staff and laity. They employ the art of asking strong questions and are prone to delve deeply from a place of curiosity.

These pastors hold the firm conviction that staff and laity are creative, resourceful, and whole, and therefore are capable of leading astonishing ministry with amazing results. Coach-approach pastors focus prodigious attention on action planning, goal setting, and accountability. Thus, staff and laity are enabled to take responsibility for their work instead of relying on the pastor to take over when challenges arise.

The coach-approach pastor values the fact that every disciple of Jesus has a calling to be in ministry. When given the chance to live out that calling, staff and laity experience greater fulfillment as disciples. The role of the clergyperson then is not only to do ministry, but also to equip the staff and laity for ministry.

> **The coach-approach pastor values the fact that every disciple of Jesus has a calling to be in ministry.**

Coaching Church Staff

In the large church, the coach-approach lead pastor interacts with staff as partners in creating ministry. Instead of seeing the lead pastor as the go-to person with the answers, the staff experience their questions being turned back to them more often with, "Let's start with what you think we should do about this situation."

> **Your typical congregation is one of least accountable organizations in the world.**

This pastor also meets with each staff person at the beginning of the church year specifically to assist him or her in establishing measurable goals for the next twelve months that align with the purpose of the church and priorities set by the congregation. The coach-approach pastor then schedules to meet at least quarterly with each staff person to measure progress toward the completion of established goals.

In the quarterly meetings, the leader asks:

- "Is this goal still important for your work and the church's ministry?"
- "If 100 percent represents completion of this goal, what percentage are you at now?"
- "What are your next steps in completing this goal?"
- "What assistance, if any, do you need from me?"

The key step in any goal development is accountability, and your typical congregation is one of least accountable organizations in the world. Without accountability, goals tend to remain wishful aspirations.

The coach-approach lead pastor exhibits sufficient fortitude to hold the staff accountable for following through with their goals and commitments. This step of accountability from the lead pastor is so important because the God-sized things in ministry habitually get sidelined due to the tyranny of the urgent and the onslaught of email. Holding staff members responsible for progress on those things that matter most adds the starch most congregational systems need to function purposefully.

The God-sized things in ministry habitually get sidelined due to the tyranny of the urgent and the onslaught of email.

I hope it is obvious that the lead pastor also must set his or her own specific and measurable goals for ministry and be held accountable for the progress toward those goals by the personnel committee in the church. In doing so, the pastor not only models good practice for the rest of the staff, but personally benefits from having the same level of accountability the rest of the staff is held to.

Coaching Lay Leadership

In the same way a coach-trained pastor meets with staff, he or she also meets individually with key lay leaders and takes a coaching posture in partnering with them.

The pastor meets with each committee or team leader annually to help plan for the coming year by asking the following questions.

- "Let's fast forward to the end of this next 12 months; what are two key things that need to happen in your area of ministry?"
- "What will it take to get those done and who would be your closest allies?"
- "What is needed from your committee or team?"
- "What do you need from me?"
- "Why is this important to the ministry of our church and how does it connect to our purpose?"

The pastor then schedules a quarterly meeting with each leader, focusing on the progress toward those goals. Pastors working so impactfully from a coaching posture with laity might then be required to attend fewer committee meetings themselves.

Coach Approach to Preaching

One of my favorite phrases learned in seminary is *hermeneutical leap* —the application of God's message through the preacher to the daily lives of those listening from the pews. Hermeneutics is the science of interpreting scripture; the leap connects the interpretation of the biblical narrative with how we are to live our daily lives.

On a weekly basis, good preaching must answer the fundamentally powerful question, "So what?" Let's say the focus of the Sunday sermon is the twelve tribes of Israel. Okay, so what? What do you want me to do differently in my life because of this message? The coach approach to preaching is intentional about bridging the hermeneutical leap from God's Word to our lives.

On a weekly basis, good preaching must answer the fundamentally powerful question, "So what?"

In addition, preachers can take a more explicit coach approach in the delivery of the Sunday sermon by ending each message with a powerful question or challenge to the congregation.

Here are some examples:

- "What might be different next Sunday if, long before you arrived for worship, you spent an hour in spiritual preparation to engage God's Word?"
- "I challenge you to introduce yourself to one person this week using these words: 'I am a Christian.'"
- "I request that over the next two days you ponder this question: 'How much am I willing to risk in support of my Muslim neighbors?' I would love for you to text me your answers by Wednesday."
- "What slight adjustment are you willing to make in your daily life to be a better steward of God's environment?"

Coach-Approach Pastoral Care

Taking the coach approach to ministry can also reshape how a pastor approaches other aspects of ministry, such as pastoral care. Here are two applications of coaching to caregiving.

Premarital Coaching

Most pastors require engaged couples to attend a series of preparation meetings prior to the wedding. We typically refer to this series as premarital counseling. What if we called it premarital coaching, and what if the pastor intentionally took more of a coach-approach to these sessions?

Here are some examples of different kinds of questions that might be asked:

- "Describe how you are as a couple when things are going really well in your relationship."
- "When you are in conflict, what slight adjustment in communication are you willing to make out of love for your partner?"
- "In what way is your marriage not just a gift to the two of you and your friends and family, but to the larger world we live in?"
- "Can I challenge you to write down some thoughts about a 'Mission Statement' for your marriage before our next session?"

My suspicion is that just the name change to premarital coaching would put couples more at ease from the beginning. And the time investment would be even more valuable if they experienced these sessions as a time of self-discovery about one another and an unfolding of the possibilities for their relationship.

End-of-Life Coaching

A great deal of the pastoral work during a person's final stage of life is providing support for the person who is dying and also to their family. The teaching dimension of this support is helping all who are involved know more about what to expect in the dying process, and the pastoral component is helping them move through the stages of death and dying. Coaching support can also be extremely helpful at this time.

There are some coaches who work through hospice by providing a specialty in end-of-life coaching. As pastors, they can provide pastoral support where needed, but they are also trained in the coach-approach to dying, which they can use in situations where it is appropriate.

The end-of-life coach asks daring questions like:

- "What would a really extraordinary last few months for you look like?"
- "How intentional do you want to be in the remaining time you have about the legacy you are leaving for others?"
- "From whom do you need to seek forgiveness and how would you do that?"
- "In your experience, who has modeled the dying process really well, and what did that look like?"
- "How might your final chapter be the amazing exclamation point God intends it to be?"

8

LAITY COACHES

Most of the resources expended by denominational offices go to develop the leadership skills of clergy. Some judicatories offer workshops to help laity lead well in specific administrative areas of responsibility such as personnel, trustees, or finance.

But overall development of leadership skills for laity is generally quite limited in conferences and judicatories. One huge untapped opportunity in congregational life is for laity to be exposed to the basic skills of coaching as a way of leading in their local church and ministry.

> **One huge untapped opportunity in congregational life is for laity to be exposed to the basic skills of coaching as a way of leading.**

A Powerful Vision

Imagine laity who consistently lead meetings using the coach-approach skills by asking probing questions, expanding possibilities through brainstorming, and getting the team or committee to commit to an action plan with specific steps, outcomes, and accountabilities.

Imagine a conference lay leader meeting individually with the lay leaders of local congregations for the purpose of coaching them around setting goals for their ministry in their local congregations. And then imagine the ripple effect of those local congregational lay leaders going back to meet with each of the key leaders in their church to help committee chairpersons set ministry goals for the year.

Ministry Is the Work of the People

A sad byproduct of the professionalization of the vocation of minister has been the expectation it created among pastors and laity that the clergy are now paid to do much of the ministry. As the clergy increasingly came to be considered hired ministry professionals, laity responsibility diminished in some meaningful aspects of ministry such as visitation, teaching, facilitating small groups, and worship leadership. Somewhere in the process, we domesticated the laity.

Somewhere in the process, we domesticated the laity.

RUMINATION

Rev. Dede Roberts, trained coach, director of the Center for Vitality, the Arkansas Annual Conference of the United Methodist Church

Coaching and coach training have breathed fresh life into many of our clergy as they have reconnected to the voice deep within — the One that called and their own response. The mystic in me sees this as one voice at the core of our being. Coaching trusts that the voice is there, the resources lie within, and we can find our way. Moreover, as trained coaches use these skills in their ministry, they are discovering that laity too have passionate callings on their lives, and ministry is being expanded beyond "what the preacher does." My continuing hope is that coaching will create generative relationships among clergy, with laity, and for the sake of the world, so we can fulfill our mission of making disciples of Jesus Christ for the transformation of the world.

Though we commonly think of liturgy as the words and flow of the worship experience on Sunday morning, the literal meaning of the word liturgy is *work of the people*. The liturgy of the congregation is laity who are fully engaged in all aspects of the meaningful work of ministry outside of Sunday worship.

One way to give the work of ministry back to the people is for pastors to more fully embrace their role as equippers of the saints by doing more to train the laity. For too long we have been asking laity to step up to provide leadership without offering them the training which prepares them to excel in their roles, sometimes essentially setting them up to fail.

It's past time for conference-level training resources to be extended beyond the clergy. It is time for us to provide leadership skill training to the laity. Basic coach-approach skill training for laity is a strategic place to start.

Laity Coaching Clergy

Laity who coach frequently bring a wide array of life experience to the coaching relationship. Many have expertise in areas that can be helpful in the church such as business development, marketing, or management, and they are able to ask questions other coaches might not know to ask.

Even though confidentiality is central to the coaching relationship, some clergy feel more comfortable being coached by a layperson who is not a peer in their profession and will never become their ministry supervisor. They feel more at ease to share their complete self and most troublesome challenges.

Some clergy feel more comfortable being coached by a layperson who ... will never become their ministry supervisor.

I recently spoke with a lay coach who has clients who are clergy as well as secular clients from corporations. He articulated a surprising irony. The clergy he coaches are commonly working on secular issues like improving technology, strengthening communication, and managing teams. The secular leaders he coaches are working on "meaning of life" issues related to faith, values, and significance. Laity bring a wide range of giftedness to the work of coaching.

RUMINATION

Claire O. Bowen, trained coach, Claire Bowen and Company, Atlanta, Georgia

The Methodist tradition centers on laity and clergy as partners
in ministry. Sitting in our pews are men and women with
years of business and management experience. Their
experience can help their clergy build teams, support pastors

in finding better life-work balance, and encourage the art of leadership.

I am a layperson who coaches clergy. The coaching skills I learned gave me structure, boundaries, and a set of tools that made me realize, "Oh, I've been doing this for years, but at times I've 'colored outside the lines.'" Simply put, even though I had the background to coach, I sometimes strayed beyond the boundaries of coaching and into consulting ... and sometimes I slipped directly into know-it-all territory.

Coach training has taught me not to overly advise clergy when coaching them. I now refrain (on good days) from leading them toward what I think is best for them. I've learned that a question such as, "What ideas do you have for bringing more of what you want into your life?" works better than "Why don't you try this!" When clergy are encouraged rather than pushed, their energy follows their best desires.

9

COACHING CLERGY

Pastors, priests, rabbis, and imams are searching out coaches to help them strengthen their leadership, balance their lives, and lead congregational transformation. As the discipline of coaching gains credibility among clergy, there is an opportunity for coaches to meet this growing demand.

Not All Clergy Are Coachable

Coaching was first used several decades ago by companies to try to help their lowest performing employees bring their quality of work up to speed. This didn't work. Corporations quickly learned this application of coaching was ineffective for two reasons: the employee must possess a basic level of job proficiency and aptitude, and that person must want to be coached. Job proficiency and a proactive willingness are the base stock in the recipe of coaching.

Today coaching is widely utilized in corporations, especially for individuals on the fast track to promotion or leaders transitioning to positions of greater responsibility. In 2017, some 900 respondents to the Sherpa Institute's twelfth annual Executive Coaching Survey reported that 35 percent of their senior managers had received coaching, and 29 percent of top executives received coaching in the last year.[1]

Today coaching is widely utilized in corporations, especially for individuals on the fast track to promotion.

According to coach Carol Goldsmith,

> No longer is coaching just a C-suite perk. For much of its 20-year history, coaching in organizations had been reserved for the CEO, COO, CIO, and other chief officers who sit at the pointy part of the plane. Now coaching is being "democratized." More than 40% of respondents to the American Management Association's Global Coaching Survey reported that coaching is being used at all leadership levels—from managers on up.[2]

Working across various denominations, the Holmes Coaching Group has noticed that about one-fifth of clergy are early adopters of innovative ideas and are highly effective wherever they serve in ministry. Coaching can help to increase their effectiveness, although it will not be the leading determinant of overall success. These leaders are just naturally gifted and are going to thrive anyway.

At the other end of the spectrum, one-fifth of clergy seem to be burned out, angry, or just causing trouble each place they serve. This group is largely not coachable. In fact, this is the last group to merit the benefit of having a coach. Instead, strategic managers place these clergy in maintenance settings to minimize the harm they can cause, supervise them, or initiate the procedure to help them find another career.

If one-fifth of clergy are inherently highly effective and one-fifth are minimally effective, what of the middle 60 percent? The large middle group of pastors between these extremes are the ones who most benefit from leadership coaching.

Characteristics of Coachable Clergy

Coachable clergy are pastors who are facing a challenge and seeking help. They engage a coach when transferring to a new ministry setting, attempting to grow a church to the next level, or desiring to move beyond feeling stuck in some aspect of life or ministry.

Coachable clergy are pastors who are facing a challenge and seeking help.

Coachable clergy serve churches of all sizes. They are generally gifted for the work of ministry and respected by their peers. They are resourceful and self-reliant, but they also pursue the input of others. They are pastors who are looking for a conversation companion who will help them on a path of discovery.

What Can Coaching Offer Leaders?

Clergy in the middle 60 percent discussed above are not typically resistant to leading substantial change—they just need some assistance in figuring out how to bring that change about. More than consulting or mentoring, the discipline of coaching is having impact in the ongoing development of leadership proficiency in the church.

Exceptional leaders are not born; they are shaped. This is true even for individuals exhibiting remarkable leadership at a young age. Along their journey, mentors and colleagues, friends and family pour into their life. Synagogues or churches, schools, and civic organizations provide growth opportunities. Employers recognize their commitment and potential and invest in their development. Leaders are molded beyond whatever natural leadership acuity they were born with.

Exceptional leaders are not born; they are shaped.

John Ortberg claims, "Leadership is the art of disappointing people at a rate they can stand."[4] A coach can help a leader determine that rate of disappointment and still remain an effective agent of change.

Over a season of coaching, a pastoral leader will typically get clearer on the God-sized changes needed in the ministry setting, get more strategically focused in his or her work, and become appreciably more courageous in leading change. Many become the leaders that they have aspired to be and that their congregations need them to be.

"Leadership is the art of disappointing people at a rate they can stand."

—JOHN ORTBERG

Coaching Encourages

Most clergy never attended a course in seminary about how to be a transformational leader. Yet bold, steady, and insightful leadership through change is what is now required of clergy serving most congregations. Providing that congregational leadership requires a tremendous amount of fortitude. This was true of Pastor Kato, who hired a coach when she began working with a new congregation.

Pastor Kato knew the changes that needed to take place for her congregation to meet the challenges of a growing membership and shrinking budget. She engaged a coach to help her think through just how to make those modifications. With the coach's help, she developed a specific plan along with an accompanying strategy for sharing the plan with her key leadership.

The modifications did not unfold exactly as she had envisioned as the congregation supported only two of the three changes. But as the pastor and congregational leadership together experienced positive results from the two approved changes, discussions turned to the possibility of making even more substantial changes for the future. Something about doing this vital work with the help of a coach at her side increased Pastor Kato's confidence as she led her congregation with steady competence.

Bold, steady, and insightful leadership through change is what is now required of clergy serving most congregations.

Coaching provides a place for critical leadership conversations to occur in the context of creative thinking and possibility. People being coached experience having a confidential dialogue partner, advocate, champion, and encourager always nudging them toward action and accountability.

Coaching Helps Clarify Matters

The challenge of changing a complex volunteer system can leave pastors uncertain about where to begin. It's difficult to be a decisive leader when your starting point is unclear. Coaches help clergy sort things out.

We encourage pastors to talk things through out loud while we ask probing questions. We invite them to see their situation from the "balcony" or "steeple" view as a way of gaining overall perspective. We assist in the process of untangling the issues so the challenges become individually more manageable. And we help them set priorities about what needs to happen first and what can wait till later.

It's difficult to be a decisive leader when your starting point is unclear. Coaches help clergy sort things out.

RUMINATION

Rev. Aaron Bouwens, trained coach, director of Vital Congregations in the Upper New York Annual Conference of the United Methodist Church

> *After years of training clergy through methods and practices long used in the church, our conference became increasingly aware that the needed results were not being found though these practices. Therefore, a new way of coming alongside clergy for growth and development was sought. Coaching has been one of the clear changes bringing about the impact and change in clergy leadership that we have been seeking.*

*We started small, training only a few as coaches, and deploying
them strategically with clergy that are in the middle 60 to 70
percent who can flourish through the benefit of coaching. Early
returns showed a coaching approach to clergy leadership
development was bearing fruit.*

*Soon we trained additional coaches and began to weave coaching
into leadership development in many areas of training. Two
areas of ministry, New Faith Communities and our Leadership
Academy, utilize coaching to the greatest level.*

*The pastors in the Leadership Academy have become advocates for
coaching as a result of their experience. We found an increase
in transfer of learning due to engagement of a coaching
relationship. Some participants reported being skeptical of
coaching at first; later they celebrated the journey of having a
coach. A significant number of participants continued their
coaching relationship after the conclusion of the Leadership
Academy.*

*Through New Faith Communities and the Leadership Academy,
the Upper New York Conference is beginning to see a culture of
coaching take root among the clergy.*

Coaching Promotes a Balanced Lifestyle

A recurrent theme we see as we coach pastors is their desire to set
boundaries around work so that other important aspects of life can
be honored. For clergy, ministry is not a job or even a profession. It
is a calling God has placed on their lives. By necessity, clergy work
most weekdays and weekends, and the majority feel a nagging
sense of guilt because they are never able to meet all the needs of
their congregation.

I do not believe God called clergy to ministry with the intention that they live woefully one-dimensional lives. A coach might help a pastor reserve days on their calendar for family and fun, develop a routine for exercise, prioritize a summer vacation, or carve out some white space.

I do not believe God called clergy to ministry with the intention that they live woefully one-dimensional lives.

Conventional watercolor artists never use the color white; they don't even own a tube of it. They are uniquely committed among artists to the creative use of white space, where, instead of applying paint to every inch of the page, they preserve portions of actual unpainted areas of the paper.

Through coaching, I have found a corresponding principle: A colorful life is usually punctuated by white space. I am referring to meditation, prayer, hammock time, quiet time, and just being. It is time without the smart phone, social media, or TV. Many of us are drowning in overstimulation from color filling every square inch of the pages of our lives. The color itself is not bad; in fact, it is beautiful. But it is overpowering without the white space, in the same way that the words printed on this page would be overwhelming without the blank space between words and paragraphs and around the margins of the page.

Many of us are drowning in the overstimulation of color filling every square inch of the pages of our lives.

RUMINATION

Rev. Vicki Loflin Johnson, trained coach, retired, Mississippi Annual Conference

I watched my two-year-old granddaughter try to force a triangle into the square opening of an old-fashioned shape-sorter. Harder and harder she pushed. In frustration, she threw down the triangle. Later, with encouragement, she tried again with a circle. At first, she pushed hard in the wrong place. Then she relaxed just a bit and … seemingly by chance, she moved her little hand toward the circle opening. When the shape slipped through, she looked up with delighted surprise.

Something similar happens in life when we try too hard to make something happen. We can muscle our way through a challenging time only to discover that the harder we push, the more resistance we feel. Cultivating white space is about learning to balance effort and surrender.

In my ongoing commitment to live and work creatively, I increasingly value a stance I have come to understand as radical receptivity. There is a larger Source of insight and energy at work in our world that we may easily fail to access. Many clergy are trapped in cycles of over-efforting and overthinking. Our minds are never still and receptive. Even when we pray, we strive to impose our to-do list on reality and on God. This is an exhausting way to live.

White space is a place of extreme openness where all judgment is suspended in favor of simply receiving. It is not so much about what we do (physical activity, family time, recreation, prayer) as it is about practicing moments when we learn to surrender our agenda. Spiritual and physical disciplines can be approached with a detailed schedule of expectations or with a willingness to be surprised. Whatever practices you choose for renewal and restoration, I invite you to intentionally release your ego's demanding expectations and cultivate a state of receptivity. Watch and wait for the way of grace.

Balanced living is more than something coaches help others claim and maintain; it is what coaches too must claim for their own lives to be their best for others. Perhaps more so than any other type of work, coaching requires spiritual, mental, and emotional health. It is almost impossible to show up for another person, to be fully present and listen at the deepest level possible, if we ourselves are coming from a life that is out of balance and feeling off-kilter.

Perhaps more so than any other type of work, coaching requires spiritual, mental, and emotional health.

Coaching Provides Spiritual Nourishment

Ironically, another area that many clergy have a hard time valuing with consistency is some form of personal spiritual discipline, such as daily devotions and prayer. These disciplines keep religious leaders rooted in their relationship to God and grounded in ministry, yet can become external, rote, and stale. Brainstorming with a coach can uncover new patterns to nourish spiritual life. One pastor combined a morning walk with praying for her congregation rather than praying from a chair in her office. Another began uploading good sermons to listen to while driving. And still another committed to dance to praise music while fixing dinner— two things he loved to do and in which he experienced God's presence.

Author John Updike writes, "What art offers is space—a certain breathing room for the spirit."[5] A good coach can help clergy create breathing room for the spirit in their daily patterns of living.

A good coach can help clergy create breathing room for the spirit in their daily patterns of living.

The Amazing Privilege

Finally, let me say what a humbling invitation it is to walk alongside a clergy leader from the stance of a coach. It is no small thing to be so trusted. The work of these leaders matters greatly in the kingdom and deserves the very best coaching available.

Notes

1. Carol Goldsmith, "Ten Trends Driving Organizational Coaching," last accessed March 20, 2018, https://libraryofprofessionalcoaching.com/concepts/strategy/future-of-coaching/ten-trends-driving-organizational-coaching/5/.
2. Carol Goldsmith, "Ten Trends Driving Organizational Coaching," last accessed March 20, 2018, https://libraryofprofessionalcoaching.com/concepts/strategy/future-of-coaching/ten-trends-driving-organizational-coaching/4/.
3. John Ortberg—Quotable Quote—Quotes," Quotes, Goodreads, last accessed March 20, 2018, https://www.goodreads.com/quotes/680427-leadership-is-the-art-of-disappointing-people-at-a-rate.
4. "John Updike Quotes," Quotes, Brainy Quote, last accessed

March 20, 2018,
https://www.brainyquote.com/quotes/john_updike_1041
28.

10

PARADOX OF THE SOULFUL SUPERVISOR

Our old institutional wineskins can no longer hold new wine. The Divine Vintner is creating something new as it becomes increasingly clear that our models for supervision in ministry must evolve to meet the needs of the current contexts and purposes of ministry.

> **Our old institutional wineskins can no longer hold new wine.**

Programming in Isolation No Longer Works

For over forty years, denominations have taken the programming approach to resourcing pastors and congregations. We have provided weeklong seminars and Saturday workshops and have brought in resourcing experts to share ideas and foster ministry.

We now realize that the limitation of the program approach to resourcing ministry is that a relatively small percentage of pastors and congregations attend those opportunities. In the Baltimore-Washington Conference of the United Methodist Church, we recognized that about 30 percent of churches and pastors take advantage of the major training that is offered, and they are repeat attenders. This means that nearly 70 percent of the churches and pastors do not take advantage of the learning opportunities provided.

What is more, those workshops rarely lead to significant congregational transformation. The actionable follow-through from most of the training provided is actually weak. It is one thing for a pastor, or a pastor with a team of laypeople, to attend an inspiring workshop. It is another thing to go back to the congregation and actually implement needed changes. Most leaders who attend seminars and workshops are not just looking for information or inspiration; they are looking for transformation.

> **Most leaders who attend seminars and workshops are not just looking for information or inspiration; they are looking for transformation.**

Which is why some judicatories are now providing short-term follow-up coaching as a part of the training events and workshops they provide. For example, the Arkansas Annual Conference provides annual funding to send a certain number of congregational leadership teams to attend a major out-of-state conference. However, part of the commitment made by each team is to engage with a conference-trained coach upon returning to help apply the new ideas gleaned from the conference. Without the additional step of coaching for implementation, the training event largely serves the purpose of inspiration but not of application.

Because judicatory leaders control portions of the budget available for workshops, seminars, and training, why would one ever expend funds to hold those events without providing access to follow-up coaching for implementation from trained coaches afterward? If transformation is the desired outcome, the training will be purposefully followed by coaching—and sometimes, that coaching can be offered by a supervisor.

A Complex Challenge

There are very few secular leadership positions anymore that allow a supervisor to function in a singular role. The complexity of the workplace demands leadership proficiency in multiple modalities along with an adaptive style of supervision. In the United Methodist denomination, those who provide supervision and oversight to ministers are called district superintendents.

In 2005, the Lewis Center for Church Leadership of Wesley Theological Seminary published a study showing these new middle-level denominational leaders identified the following as the skills in which they most need to grow to function well in their new positions:

1. Coaching congregations toward growth and renewal
2. Conflict management
3. Supervision[1]

The second two skills relate most directly to the traditional management role of a supervisor, while the first is the leverage point that focuses on strategy and transformation. This explains why our coach training for denominational leaders has been in such demand across the country since we started offering it in 2010. While denominational leaders are varyingly gifted, most are eager to enhance their overall aptitude—not only in coaching, but also in the whole cluster of identified skills used by coaches.

RUMINATION

Dr. Varlyna Wright, trained coach, retired, former district superintendent of the Capital District in the Greater New Jersey Annual Conference of the United Methodist Church

> *Coaching as a district superintendent makes the job of superintending more joyful and purposeful for me.*

> *Supervision with soul is coaching while watching how God is working to transform the life and ministry of a willing and ready clergyperson. There is a real sacredness about coaching when the pastor begins to see himself or herself as a whole, resourceful, and creative person.*

> *Coaching allowed me the opportunity to develop deeper relationships with clergy that would not have been possible when I was functioning as their authoritative supervisor.*

> *Coaching enabled me to be intentional about assisting clergy in discovering or rediscovering their potential for greater effectiveness in ministry.*

At an interdenominational national gathering focused on bringing about change in religious institutions, I had the honor of representing the discipline of coaching. The panel of which I was a part also included a top church consultant and a nationally-known spiritual director. We were given the task of delineating the uniqueness of each of our helping modalities and enumerating their strengths.

I described to the gathering how I coached pastors who were also under my direct supervision. And as you might imagine, during the question and answer period, I received a considerable amount of pushback for breaking what is thought to be a sacrosanct rule of coaching: "You cannot be both a person's supervisor and coach."

Finally, an Australian coach from the back of the room stood up. In a commanding voice, he declared, "I beg to differ with the argument everyone else is making. I think you've got it exactly right! This notion that you've got to segment roles and be only one thing to a person under your leadership is rubbish. If a supervisor can supervise when needed, instruct when required, counsel when asked, and coach when coaching is appropriate, that supervisor is playing the most helpful roles imaginable for team members. By adding coaching to your supervision of clergy, you've got it exactly right!"

"This notion that you've got to segment roles and be only one thing to a person under your leadership is rubbish."

—AUSTRALIAN COACH

We did learn that the coach approach to the ministry of supervision would become the most frequently utilized tool in the supervisor's tool belt and the one that had the greatest helpful impact on pastors and congregations. In my case, coaching became the tool the clergy under my supervision most often requested from me.

In one United Methodist conference where superintendents and clergy peers have been properly trained as coaches, when a pastor requests a coach and is given a list of coaches comprised of their peers and also including their superintendent, a surprising number select their superintendent to be their coach.

Adaptive Work

Remaining static in the role of supervision and leadership is no longer a choice. Our "species" must adapt.

> **Remaining static in the role of supervision and leadership is no longer a choice. Our "species" must adapt.**

Technical problems are solved by following a known response, which is often written as protocol. With adaptive challenges, there are no experts and no easy fixes so the leader has to discern a way forward using innate wisdom. Most of what happens in ministry and the supervision of pastors these days requires a high degree of adaptive (rather than technical) leadership. Ministry in our time has more in common with hang gliding than with flying a commercial airplane; it is more like improv than scripted acting.

During this time in the life of the church, which requires such a high degree of adaptive leadership, coaching is the most effective tool available in the superintending tool kit.

> **Coaching is the most effective tool available in the superintending tool kit.**

Managing Power

Authentic relationship is the only "agency" we have in coaching. At the same time, it would be imprudent to ignore the dynamics of power at play in every relationship. This is especially true when a supervisor is coaching a person who reports to him or her. The power inequity can affect how safe the client feels and can also create a tendency for the person to defer to, or want to please, the coach. As a supervisor who also coached pastors under my supervision, I had to earn every inch of the pastor's trust in order to coach effectively. With some pastors, I never did earn their trust.

> **Authentic relationship is the only "agency" we have in coaching.**

In his succinct and helpful article "Coaching and Power," Robert Gass lifts up three kinds of power that may be present in a coaching relationship.

- Cultural power in which the coach and the client come from different ethnic or social backgrounds holding differing levels of privilege, or lack thereof.
- Professional power where, by virtue of being the "helper," the coach is seen as having more expertise or authority, and the client has less power as the one being helped.
- Positional power, which we are discussing here, where the coach is also the supervisor.[3]

> **"The reality that coaching takes place in a context of power should not be viewed as a problem."**
>
> —ROBERT GASS

Gass maintains, "The reality that coaching takes place in a context of power should not be viewed as a problem." However, he suggests the coach can take steps to mitigate the impact of the power imbalance. Here are two suggestions for doing so.

First, when coaching across cultural lines, make sure you have done your own solid work to increase your sensitivity and awareness around intercultural competencies. This is especially true for coaches coming from backgrounds that have been afforded greater privilege in society.

As a tall, heterosexual Caucasian male from North America who is living in relative affluence, my experience of the world and others' experience of me in the world is markedly different from people who do not share those same layers of privilege. The experience would be even more influenced if I were coaching people whom I supervise. It would be naïve to think otherwise.

Coaching should never be used as a means of learning about another culture. The coach must do his or her own work around intercultural competencies and not expect the pastor to be the teacher. Most denominations offer specific training in these competencies and offer assessments to help identify blind spots. The goal is always to interact with sensitivity and awareness. Greater self-understanding can help keep a coach from being unwittingly harmful in the coaching relationship.

Greater self-understanding can help keep a coach from being unwittingly harmful in the coaching relationship.

Second, consider talking about the potential or inherent issues of power with persons you are coaching. It is reasonable to bring up the subject of power at the outset of a coaching relationship so that together you can design a way to manage those challenges. The issue of power can actually be brought up for mutual reflection at any point in the process of coaching.

Admittedly, Robert Gass's article is written from a privileged white male perspective. I have yet to read an article written on the subject of power and coaching from the perspective of a non-majority person of color. I look forward to someday reading that article because it is needed in this field.

RUMINATION

Dr. Youngsook Charlene Kang, associate certified coach, Director of Mission and Ministry and the Clergy Peer Coaching Network in the Rocky Mountain Conference of the United Methodist Church, former district superintendent of the Metropolitan District of the Rocky Mountain Conference.

> *Intercultural competence is the ability to effectively communicate and appropriately relate with people in cross-cultural contexts. Intercultural competence is about diversity and inclusion. Diversity is the reality of cultural differences, and inclusion is an intentional effort to make this diversity work.*

> *Why is Intercultural competence important? In essence, coaching relationships span many differences—gender, age, sexuality, and profession. As the world becomes more and more global, ethnicity and race are increasingly important influencing factors for coaches to be aware of. Ethnicity and race are increasingly important parts of coaching relationships as the world is becoming more and more diverse and global.*

> *Intercultural competence serves as a powerful tool for sustainable success in coaching relationships because it enhances an understanding of one's own cultural orientations and values. Effective intercultural coaching opens the doors to a wider and deeper understanding of the person's issues and background. It enables one to reach the internal self under the waterline of the cultural iceberg. Therefore, intercultural competence as a coaching skill increases the ability to better understand the*

individual's intuition and imagination. have taken the IDI to improve intercultural competence.

Stay in Your Lane

If a denominational leader is going to intentionally function in a variety of helpful capacities, that leader must be clear about the role he or she is standing in at any given time. It is unfair and confusing to the other person if the leader is coaching one moment, directing the next, and then supervising after that, all in the same conversation.

While it is best for a supervisor to stay in a singular mode of interaction during a conversation, if we do decide to switch functions, we must use our blinker when switching lanes.

Just like our driving instructors taught us, it is reckless to swerve in and out of lanes without using the signal indicator. In changing roles, the leader might say, "Can I remove my coaching hat for a moment to make a suggestion? Or do you mind if I switch to my supervisor mode for a moment?"

Supervision with Soul

To supervise soulfully is to let go of the singular role limitation of supervision and to be willing to lean in to the leadership role that utilizes a variety of skills to be helpful to others, including coaching. Bring ingenuity and creativity to the artful work of leadership. Be fair with those you supervise about the role you are taking in relation to them in a given moment. And do all you can to increase your intercultural competency and to acknowledge and manage the power dynamics present in the coaching relationship, all for the purpose of being the very best leader you can be for those God has called you to serve. This is supervising with soul.

To supervise soulfully is to let go of the singular role limitation of supervision.

Multidisciplinary Art Form

If you are a supervisor, challenge yourself to imagine your job more as a multidisciplinary art form and less as a mono functioning management role. Your denominational leadership position requires a great deal more from you than supervisory middle management. As my friend Bishop Bill McAlilly says, "Superintendents have accepted a dangerous opportunity."[2] What is needed now from those in supervisory positions is adaptive, strategic, and innovative leadership that includes the ability to coach clergy and laity directly and to embrace the coach approach to leading in general.

What is needed now from those in supervisory positions is adaptive, strategic, and innovative leadership that includes the ability to coach.

Here are some examples of what it might look like for a denominational supervisor who has had coach training to integrate the power of coaching.

Individual Coaching

- Offer individual coaching to each of the new pastors under your guidance for the first six months. This could be as casual as a monthly breakfast conversation or a scheduled coaching phone call.

- Select five gifted pastors who are doing strategic work with their congregations that has resulted in transformational change. Look for the ones with bright and eager eyes. Offer to meet with each one individually, or as a group or both, to offer your coaching support.
- Offer to coach key laity or youth and young adults who are contemplating ministry.

Group Coaching

- Offer to meet as a group with new pastors and use the coach approach to mine the peer learning from the group; do some targeted coaching of one individual in the group along the way. This requires the leader to remain inquisitive, taking an asking approach to the conversation rather than an authoritative telling approach.
- Identify pastors who have a common strategic goal, such as breaking the 100 or 200 or 500 barriers in average worship attendance, or who are leading through congregational merger, or who are starting building programs, or tactically downsizing, or starting new small groups or new community-related ministries. Maximize the built-in affinity these pastors have with one another by coaching them forward as a group.
- Develop a culture of coaching by getting six to ten respected pastors trained in coaching so they can utilize coaching skills with their clergy peers.

Select five gifted pastors who are doing strategic work with their congregations … Look for the ones with bright and eager eyes.

Four Good Questions

In all the teaching I have done with denominational leaders, there is one thing that leaders have most dependably captured in their notes. It is the four good questions for a leader to ask from a supervisory position.

- What can we celebrate that has gone well?
- Where are you stuck?
- What, if anything, do you need from me?
- How may I pray for you?

Countless denominational leaders have reported to me the difference it made when they adopted these questions as the format for their annual one-on-one meetings with clergy. The response has been similar from lead pastors who use them individually with their staff or lay chairpersons, bishops using them with their members of their leadership team, and lay leaders using them with leaders of ministries initiatives.

RUMINATION

Rev. Steven Coburn, trained coach, district superintendent of the Northwest District in the Arkansas Conference of the United Methodist Church

> *Your four questions of "celebrate, stuck, need, and prayers" have provided a great template for use in my annual clergy assessment conversations. I find the four questions to be similar to the model of "Loving, Leading, and Learning." This coach-approach conversation allows me to be more of a guide as opposed to an administrator. The conversation celebrates ministry while also probing ways to maximize clergy strengths*

rather than failures/weakness. The result is deeper trust, more authentic conversation, and a stronger relationship with clergy.

The last question, "How may I pray for you," fully honors the spiritual dimension of the relationship supervisors have with those to whom they are partnered in doing God's work. It is always appropriate to offer to pray for another with whom you share ministry. If you are not making the offer to pray with pastors you supervise, there is a very good chance no one else in their circle is either.

If you are not making the offer to pray with pastors you supervise ... no one else in their circle is either.

Notes

1. Lovett H. Weems, Jr., "A District Superintendent's First Year: A Report on Research with New United Methodist District Superintendents," Lewis Center for Church Leadership of Wesley Theological Seminary, 2005, 5.
2. Bishop Bill McAlilly, Opening Worship at DS/DCM Training Event, Lake Junaluska, North Carolina, August 21, 2017.
3. Robert Gass, "Coaching and Power," *Tools for Transformation* http://stproject.org/resources/tools-for-transformation/coaching/, 100.

PART IV

APPLICATIONS OF
COACHING TO
MINISTRY SYSTEMS

11

ESTABLISHING A COACHING NETWORK

Peer coaching is the fastest-growing development in clergy coaching. Networks of coaches are popping up all over the country as an essential means to leverage clergy and laity effectiveness and move congregations toward needed transformational change. These coaches come from and are trained by their specific diocese, conference, or presbytery and then they coach other leaders within that organization. The scope of impact this coaching is having is impressive, and in my opinion the development of these networks has become, in the last two years, a nationwide movement.

Peer coaching is the fastest-growing development in clergy coaching.

You might be a Presbyterian pastor starting a new congregation in Duluth or a United Methodist pastor serving a church in the Rockies. You might be an Episcopal priest leading a congregation in downtown Savannah or a layperson in the Church of Scotland.

What each of these leaders has in common is easy access to someone who is probably already known to them, a colleague trained as a coach and skilled at helping others become the best leaders they can be.

Over the last five years, the Holmes Coaching Group has assisted in establishing internal regional coaching networks in twelve different denominational settings. Leaders of all denominations are starting to pay attention to the growing trend of internal coaching networks.

Leaders of all denominations are starting to pay attention to the growing trend of internal coaching networks.

The Purpose of Coaching Networks

Coaching networks are established for a variety of purposes. Consider both the similarity and variety of purpose espoused by the leaders of these networks.

- Alignment with our strategic purpose of investing in the leadership development of our young clergy and pastors serving in settings of diversity. We are creating an eco-system of leadership development.
- Our hope through coaching is that our leaders will develop a greater adaptive capacity, including greater courage and confidence, and an increase in risk-taking.
- Through coaching we are resourcing pastors and churches in making the next "right step" into congregational health. Using coaches who are ICF-certified is the gold standard for our presbytery.
- We are creating a culture of clergy peer coaching to help

leaders move toward greater effectiveness and accountability. We are increasing the vitality of churches and developing much-needed potential and resiliency.

- The purpose of our coaching network is to help pastors grow in their overall leadership, effectiveness, and self-care.
- We have greatly increased clergy retention by providing leaders with a coach with whom they can have confidential conversations around increased effectiveness.
- We are building the capacity of Christ-following leaders as we also heighten our connectional life together.

Application of coaching through these networks also differs. In one, coaches are coaching laity, and specifically, children's ministries coordinators in local churches. In another, individual coaching is expected for newly assigned pastors. One coaching network provides group coaching to teams of six to eight clergy and lay leaders from the same congregation; another offers theme-oriented group sessions for pastors from different congregations. Several conferences in the United Methodist Church have established a "round robin" coaching network, in which coaches from one conference provide coaching to clergy in the adjacent conference and vice versa.

Many of the internal coaching networks that focus most pointedly on increasing clergy effectiveness combine coaching with some form of assessment to measure clergy effectiveness. The most popular assessments are "360-degree tools" that gather input not only from the pastor, but also from those with whom they work most closely. The follow-up coaching then naturally focuses on what the pastor learned from the assessment results, exploring what he or she wants to begin to do differently as a result.

One conference utilizes a tool that takes into account a clergyperson's past performance as well as his or her learning agility, people agility, and results agility.

Overcoming Challenges

It may be obvious that the overriding disadvantage to establishing a peer-coaching network is the reluctance of clergy to trust one another. Many clergy see their peers as potential threats or competitors rather than as allies who can be a helpful resource.

Two strategies for mitigating this mistrust are to allow coaching only for clergy who have a desire to receive coaching, and to give them the chance to select the peer coach they want to work with. Trust and impact of the coaching increase greatly when willingness and choice are key features.

> **Trust and impact of the coaching increase greatly when willingness and choice are key features.**

Benefits of Developing a Coaching Network

Here are some of the advantages that make network coaching desirable.

- Network coaching is more affordable than hiring an outside coaching company to coach pastors. Hired coaches are present only for the length of the contract they have signed and then they are gone. Internally-trained clergy and laity coaches remain in-house often coaching at a reduced cost.
- Often (because the denomination selects, sponsors, and pays for the coaches to be trained) those coaches are expected to pay back the cost of the training by coaching their peers. This becomes a form of in-kind service to the denomination. Sometimes the coaching is provided free of charge and sometimes coaches are paid a stipend for the work they do.

- With internal coaches, the denomination is assured they have coaches with a basic understanding of the ministry context, and it is possible to tailor the coaching to be more contextual and address specific needs in ministry.
- Judicatories have a better chance of establishing a "culture of coaching" because the network of trained coaches becomes extant advocates and catalysts for coaching within the system that they are a part of. The synergy emanation from peer-coaching circles has a viral effect on the larger system.

The synergy emanating from peer coaching circles has a viral effect on the larger system.

In 2016, students being trained in coaching at Africa University in Zimbabwe by the United Methodist General Board of Global Ministries decided to form a student peer-coaching club. Students at Africa University come from over twenty different African nations. Students from seven of those nations have begun offering peer coaching to their fellow students on campus, and the impact is already making a difference in student life at this multicultural university.

In this chapter I have incorporated stories of the development of two successful, internally-formed organizational coaching models that are currently being well utilized. These stories are shared by the leaders responsible for establishing those networks. In both cases, the leaders did an excellent job of providing the explanation of how coaching would be used and of demonstrating the benefits of coaching to their whole community. There is a great deal to be learned from both examples and that can be adapted to other denominations for their contexts and purposes.

RUMINATION

The Right Reverend Scott Benhase, 10th Bishop of the Episcopal Diocese of Georgia

When I became bishop of the Episcopal Diocese of Georgia in 2010, I soon noticed that the clergy relationships were not as healthy as they should be. There was no general animosity or rampant competitiveness, nor was there any significant "bad blood" between clergy. On the contrary, there were anecdotal friendships and some trust within groups of some clergy. I sensed, however, that status quo was not optimal and it certainly was not going to help our clergy thrive in the rapidly changing landscape of the church in the twenty-first century.

Early on in my episcopate, in listening to the longings of clergy, I began to recruit clergy who showed a willingness to learn and to change behaviors. Together we mapped out the skills we saw that were needed for clergy in our various contexts in southern Georgia. They included:

(1) basic skills in how to lead people through the complex changes the church and culture were experiencing
(2) self-awareness by the clergy of how they impacted and were impacted by their leadership
(3) support and accountability for leading their respective congregations in growth and development.

To address the first point, we brought in the Church Development Institute, a leadership development program held for eight weekends over a two-year period. For the second point, we partnered with the Center for Emotional Intelligence so clergy could develop greater self-awareness around their leadership and learn how they impacted others and how others affected them. And for the third point, we worked with the Reverend Chris Holmes to develop a diocesan-wide peer-coaching program in which all clergy would participate. And to make this a long-term cultural change in the diocese, we mandated all these to be an integral part of every new letter of agreement for clergy to serve in the diocese. In other words, I would not license clergy to serve in the diocese without their buy-in to participate in all of this ongoing training.

To say the peer-coaching initiative has been a game-changer would be an understatement. Within a short time, it has helped our clergy stay focused on the important work of congregational development and not be distracted by less important but seemingly urgent aspects of parish ministry. It has imbued both focus and accountability because when clergy know they have a coach who is walking with them through their leadership challenges, they are more likely to stay with the developmental tasks. Sinners that we all are, having someone we are accountable to for the things we say we want to accomplish ... well, it makes all the difference.

The results have been wonderful. Our clergy now are more focused on what is important in their ministries. They are less distracted by what appears to be an urgent thing of the moment. Their peer coaches have helped them keep a long view to their congregational leadership while also helping them develop manageable goals that all build together toward that long view.

There has also been an unexpected (by me) spillover benefit from our peer-coaching initiative. I certainly hoped and expected it would help our clergy focus on the important developmental tasks of congregational leadership. And it has. What I had not expected, and what has delighted me, is how the peer-coaching initiative has helped transform clergy relationships within the diocese. When we now gather for our semi-annual clergy conferences, I see very little of the old animosities and unhealthy competitiveness ("mine's bigger than yours") of seven-plus years ago. To be sure, we clergy are still a collection of imperfect people serving an impossible vocation, and thus we are susceptible to the petty jealousies and envies with which all humans suffer. But that is so much less now and is almost absent. What I do see when we gather are clergy who are pulling together and pulling for one another.

The peer-coaching initiative has created friendships and relationships across a large geographical diocese. There is a gentle ease and good humor that we now share with one another. I have no doubt a good part of the transformation we have experienced is directly related to the peer coaching relationships that have been created.

Our peer-coaching initiative has not been a cure-all. If there is not a clear missional strategy being articulated and other structures put in place for the Gospel to be proclaimed and disciples to be formed, then peer coaching will not magically fill in all the gaps. But where these other important tasks are being attended to, peer coaching will be transformational.

Wisdom of the Forerunners

In March 2018, my partner, George Howard, and I hosted a conversation among the chief organizers of ten internal coaching networks from all over the country. We entitled this first-ever gathering a "Wisdom Council"—I mean really, what leaders could pass up the opportunity to participate in a Wisdom Council? Wisdom was defined by one of the participants as "the practical application of imagination that is supported by a heart that listens and a mind that learns."

Over two days, the leaders of these networks shared best practices and applications of coaching in their settings and learned from one another. Here is a summary of the highlights from our conversation.

It takes time to establish a culture of peer coaching. In fact, it takes years to establish a culture where coaching provided by peers is normative. In the longest running network, which has been in existence for seven years, pastors experiencing some form of transition in ministry placement are assigned a coach. The Diocese pays for the first twelve months of mandatory coaching. Even though they must pay for the coaching services after that, 90 percent of the people who begin with a coach voluntarily continue with a coach. In addition, the laity in this diocese are beginning to ask the clergy serving their congregation if they are taking advantage of the help of a coach. Compared to all the other leadership development resources denominations expend money on, internal coaching is highly valued and cost effective.

> **Compared to all the other leadership development resources denominations expend money on, peer coaching is … cost effective.**

On-going skill development is needed to maintain excellence. The process to become a credentialed professional coach is rigorous; however ongoing development for internal coaches is beneficial. In the places where peer coaching is being effectively utilized, there are monthly in-services, supervision, or practice opportunities for peer coaches. Often these coaches coach one another in reciprocity.

Buy-in from top leadership is critical. It is difficult to establish a coaching network within an organization when starting at the level of middle management. Internal coaching has the most impact where key decision-makers themselves have been coached and understand its value. Support from bishops and other judicatory executives is crucial. In one setting, not only the bishop receives a coach, but the organization pays for each of its twenty-nine full-time staff members to be professionally coached by coaches outside their system to help those leaders be the best leaders they can be and as a way to reinforce the value of coaching through the organization.

> **Internal coaching has the most impact where key decision-makers themselves have been coached.**

Mislabeling other helping modalities as "coaching" is harmful. The biggest offenders are the consultants and mentors who mask their services as "coaching." Compared to the other helping professions, coaching is crystal clear that the expertise lies with the person being coached, not with some outside source like a consultant or mentor. The most challenging places to establish an internal network of coaches who are valued for their competence is a setting where constituents have had a bad experience at an earlier date with a consultant who mislabeled what they were offering as "coaching."

It is necessary to be selective about recruitment of coaches. The brightest and most respected members of an organization should be recruited to be coaches in an internal coaching network. This is especially true in the first round of recruitment, which communicates a high standard of excellence and sets a baseline standard.

> The brightest and most respected members of an organization should be recruited to be coaches in an internal coaching network.

Participants should get a taste of peer coaching. When pastors or laity actually observe a person they know being coached in a live coaching demonstration, they are most likely to understand what coaching is and what it is not. Coaching demonstrations with an accompanying debrief take only thirty minutes and should be featured frequently at clergy and laity gatherings to remind leaders of the power of coaching. Those are also occasions to share the stories of success stemming from coaching relationships, or to even request a "witness" from a person who has been coached.

Coaching is tied to seminars and workshops. Another best practice is for pastors and congregational teams who are selected to attend seminars, workshops, and other professional development events also receive follow-up coaching. In other words, it is not enough to go to a continuing education event for a week and learn about new skills and concepts. Clergy must also come home and purposefully apply those new skills and concepts in their ministry context with the help of a peer coach. They are encouraged to become reflective practitioners of the new skills or concepts.

Internal coaching networks for clergy and laity are beginning to prove their staying power. They are demonstrating that much of the faithful, helpful, and deeply spiritual work occurring among church leaders today happens through peer coaching. It's no wonder these networks are starting to flourish and grow.

Much of the faithful, helpful, and deeply spiritual work occurring among church leaders today happens through peer coaching.

RUMINATION

Rev. Myrna Bethke, associate certified coach, district superintendent of the Gateway South District in the Greater New Jersey Annual Conference of the United Methodist Church

Three years ago, we began rolling out an introduction of coaching to our conference by having all of the bishop's cabinet members and the connectional ministries staff trained in coaching. They also began to be coached by a team of professional coaches. As part of their conference work, each trained staff member then began to coach up to fifteen clergypersons, with the expectation that their capacity would eventually increase to twenty-five pastors. Next, circuit leaders, who are active clergy working in each region of the conference, were trained in coaching so they could coach up to five of their peers.

We have the capacity to coach every active clergy member of the conference, but our goal was to engage 300 clergy with a coach by the end of 2017. We were very close to achieving that goal.

We got the conference-wide buy-in for coaching by using the Bishop's Convocation, held for two-and-a half days annually for clergy and spouses. The convocation is an opportunity to train clergy in the basic skills of coaching for use in ministry. Three hundred people signed up for the training, and at the end of it around 100 signed up to be coached by one of the trained conference staff. At this event clergy could really see what coaching is and what it is not. They saw that coaching wasn't something we wielded as a form of supervision, but instead was a helpful opportunity of coming alongside clergy who wanted to "up their game." We have continued to model and reinforce the benefits of coaching by integrating it into the subsequent Bishop's Convocations and conference events.

Coaching has really changed the culture of how clergy provide leadership. I have seen a change in the use of clergy language and interaction with laity since we began integrating it. Pastors no longer do so much answer giving as they do asking questions of lay leadership to bring out their gifts for ministry. Clergy are starting to ask questions like, "What would it look like if we did _____?" Through coaching our clergy are experiencing empowerment, an increase in morale, and a greater freedom to try new things. Trying something new and failing is seen as a way of learning.

We are now starting to measure our investment in coaching by reviewing the five-year progress of churches that have been led by clergy who have had experience with coaching as compared to those who have not. One of the things I hear over and over again from clergy is, "I wish I had known about coaching earlier. I wish I had been given the coach approach to ministry tools much sooner in my ministry."

COACHING ON A MASSIVE SCALE

More than a decade ago, I helped to lead and implement the most extensive peer coaching development attempted in any denomination. Over six consecutive years, eighteen trained coaches on our conference staff coached close to 700 pastors. (The original coach training I received was so I could help lead and provide direction to this tremendous experiment in the Baltimore-Washington Conference of the United Methodist Church.) In brief, here was our model.

Over six consecutive years, eighteen trained coaches on our conference staff coached close to 700 pastors.

All clergy were assigned to a group that met monthly under the leadership of a coach and used material developed by pastors working with conference staff. Each month focused on a different theme for ministry, such as "Growing Hospitality," "Connecting with the Community," or "Stewardship of God's Creation."

Each pastor also scheduled a monthly coaching call or visit with their coach, which was designed to assist him or her in moving to action on some aspect of peer-group learning or one of the God-sized goals he or she developed for their congregation.

The district I served for seven years was comprised of seventy-two congregations and roughly that many pastors. I coached thirty-two of the pastors; the others were coached by two other coach-trained staff members. About half of my group of thirty-two adapted easily to the individual coaching and utilized it well. Two pastors were not coachable; their ineffectiveness required my supervision instead. What I have described here about my district is commensurate with the model and experience of coaching provided in the other seven districts in the conference.

RESULTS

After six years of group coaching coupled with individual coaching, we ended the forty-year decline in the Annapolis district in all the quantifiable denominational measurements: average worship attendance, new members, baptisms, and levels of giving. More specifically, for the first time the aggregate number of measurable statistics for all the district congregations increased over the previous year. Two other districts that also applied the coaching model reached that goal the year before we did, and still others followed.

> **We ended the forty-year decline in all the quantifiable denominational measurements.**

In my opinion, what happened over those years of intensive conference-wide coaching is that our congregations gradually got healthier and our pastors got more focused on the hard work of congregational transformation. The increase in measurable statistics was not so much the objective as the byproduct of more purposefully focused clergy and slightly healthier churches.

> **Our congregations gradually got healthier and our pastors got more focused on the hard work of congregational transformation.**

This colossal, conference-wide coaching effort was not perfect, and we learned invaluable lessons that have helped shaping subsequent large-scale models in other conferences.

THE LEARNING

Readiness and choice are two huge factors in the efficacy of coaching.

Readiness and choice are two huge factors in the efficacy of coaching.

To say that some of the clergy in our conference did not appreciate being told their participation in group and individual coaching was expected is an understatement. A small number of clergy just refused to participate; some came reluctantly, and some had such a poor attitude about it they were asked not to continue their participation. But a larger percentage adapted and found the group and individual coaching meaningful. In a survey conducted by the conference several years into the process, 87 percent of the clergy respondents said they appreciated being a part of their peer learning groups

In hindsight, we also realized the advantage of an individual being able to choose his or her coach from a supplied list of coaches. The participant's buy-in to the coaching relationship is understandably greater when a choice of coach is provided.

Subsequently, the large-scale coaching initiatives we help to design honor readiness and choice as two primary components.

12

GROUP COACHING

Research and development in the field of group coaching is about fifteen years behind the field of individual coaching. Nevertheless, in growing numbers, coaches are coaching groups of leaders as opposed to individuals. There are a number of good reasons to consider offering coaching in this form.

Affordability and Efficiency

The first major advantage is that group coaching is comparatively affordable for participants. Individual coaching in the nonprofit arena tends to range from $125 to $175 per hour. By contrast, group coaching can cost each participant $30 to $50 per hour. While individual coaching is more the norm in corporations which can afford it, many nonprofit organizations opt for more economical group coaching.

Group coaching is comparatively affordable for participants.

Group coaching is also more time-efficient for the coach. Eight to twelve participants can be coached for an hour and receive substantial benefit. Additionally, those participants experience the synergy of learning between members of the group.

RUMINATION

Dr. Brian Brown, associate certified coach, pastor of Woodlawn-Faith Church, Virginia, former district superintendent of the Ohio River Valley District in the West Ohio Conference of the United Methodist Church

> *The district I served had 140 pastors. That meant we needed to start doing more group work with clergy and less one-on-one work. In our district, "cell groups" which were small groups of pastors, became very important.*

> *I applied for a grant that allowed me to offer the combination of group and individual coaching to a number of the clergy, many of whom were my cell group leaders who met with small groups of pastors throughout the district. The participants were basically my leadership team for the district.*

> *Several components of the group coaching were beneficial, but if I had to sum up the impact in one phrase, it would be* an increase in the trust factor. *Pastors began to feel less like lone rangers. Group coaching gave them a greater sense of tolerance when they realized that what they were going through was not unique to their situation. God honors in a special way the coming together of clergy to learn from one another.*

> *We followed the group coaching with one-on-one coaching, which gave participants a chance to talk about and process what they*

learned from the group discussion. In my opinion, there would be something missing without both components of group coaching followed by individual coaching.

Ginger Cockerham, one of the early pioneers in group coaching, believes that group coaching is preferable to individual coaching. Individuals participating in group coaching benefit from peer input and group interaction, which individual coaching does not have. Not all coaches agree with her assessment, but it is worth considering.

Individuals participating in group coaching benefit from peer input and group interaction, which individual coaching does not have.

What makes this experience group coaching as opposed to a facilitated conversation? The coach maintains the coaching stance by asking a series of probing discovery questions, and at times offers to individually coach a participant in the middle of the session while other participants observe. The final element that makes this group coaching is that the session ends with a request for a commitment to action from each member of the group.

The clearest way for me to describe the varieties of group coaching is to give an overview of three models I have developed and utilized over many years.

Coaching Clergy Groups

In 2008, I developed and began offering a clergy group coaching series that has been successfully utilized around the country. The series takes place over nine months, usually September through June with a break for Christmas.

Some conference leaders offer this opportunity to all of their clergy and allow interested clergy to sign-up, some strategically recruit participants, and still others require a written application followed by a selection process.

Sometimes the groups are formed around affinity, such as newly appointed pastors, or pastors of large congregations, or pastors attempting to change the culture of their congregations regardless of the size of the church. Pastors who are burned out and bitter or have a history of causing conflict are not eligible to participate in these groups.

Sometimes the groups are formed around affinity.

Very often the judicatory pays for half or most of the expense involved, requiring the participating clergy to share in a portion of the cost. Clergy who share the cost make better use of the coaching opportunity.

Pastors who are burned out and bitter or have a history of causing conflict are not eligible to participate.

An initial in-person meeting is held with the eight to twelve participants, which gives the coach a chance to interact with them directly, to explain and demonstrate coaching, and to answer any questions they may have. Subsequent interactions use a video interface platform over the internet.

Group sessions last ninety minutes, are highly interactive, rely on peer sharing, and are complemented by instruction from the coach. Each conversation concludes with individuals designing and committing to personalized action steps around the theme for that session.

I have offered this model of group coaching for many years now, helping hundreds of pastors become more focused in their work and more courageous and creative in their leadership.

Basic Applications of Coaching

During the initial interview, and depending on the situation, the coach might adapt the approach taken to working with an individual or a group. The three basic approaches differ by the amount of content introduced by the coach and the degree to which there is an agreed-upon focus for the conversation.

Content-free coaching offers coaching on whatever the person being coached would like the conversation to focus on. The opening coaching question is usually, "What would you like us to focus on today?"

Content-rich coaching brings a designated theme to the coaching conversation. Thus, the coaching questions relate to that theme.

Content-full coaching focuses the coaching conversation closely around certain bench marks or material that has been presented. New congregational development is often content full.

Most often, group coaching is "content rich" and is built around a selected theme for each month. Participants do pre-work for each session in the form of a worksheet and by listening to an instructional video focused on that month's theme. Some examples of possible themes include Increasing Vitality in Worship, Equipping Lay Leadership, and Connecting with Your Community.

RUMINATION

Dr. Arun Paul, trained coach, pastor of Oxford United Methodist Church, Oxford, Ohio

Over the years in my Christian ministry experience I had been a mentor, a counselor, teacher-trainer, and sometimes a consultant. However, group coaching not only informed me about the "coach approach to ministry" but I also began to use the material that I received for these sessions at my monthly leadership team meetings. Soon I realized the impact of this new approach on my church leadership team as they began to open themselves up for more discussion and further learning.

Coaching Clergy Groups Plus Individual Coaching

Another widely utilized model combines group coaching with individual coaching for each participant. Following the group session, participants sign up for a fifty-minute individual coaching session to be held with their coach later in the month. During the individual coaching the pastor fully contextualizes the group learning to the uniqueness of the ministry setting.

> During the individual coaching the pastor fully contextualizes the group learning to the uniqueness of the ministry setting.

RUMINATION

Rev. Whitney Mitchell, senior pastor of Fayetteville First United Methodist Church

> *Not long after the transition to serve on the ministry team of a large membership congregation, the district offered a group coaching experience. The group calls were filled with wisdom from my colleagues' experiences around the touchstones outlined in the videos and handouts. I especially benefited in the group calls when our coach would ask an open, honest question of us, and then coach us to accountable actions.*

> *What surprised me even more was when I spoke with my coach in my individual coaching calls. He would ask, "So, in our group call you said this about X. How's it going?" I found this to be most helpful because up until this point my experience had been that we, as pastors, like to talk big and perform little.*

> *After several of our sessions, I left feeling like I had been all talk with little action in those ministry areas, but I came away from those sessions with tools to start building the bridge of developing/coaching the ministries forward.*

The individual coaching sessions also provide an opportunity for the coach to work closely with each pastor in the development of clear goals for his or her ministry setting. Typically, pastors develop at least three specific and measurable goals, which they share with their personnel committee or judicatory leader.

Group Coaching for New Denominational Leaders

One of the most successful models for group coaching is the coaching provided for newly appointed district superintendents and directors of connectional ministry in the United Methodist Church. Annually these new middle judicatory leaders gather together for a week of training on the beautiful shores of Lake Junaluska, North Carolina.

These leaders come to learn best practices for their job, such as adequately keeping personnel files, effectively processing formal complaints against clergy, dealing with legal matters, tracking candidates for ministry, and basically how not to screw things up in this new role. They are also challenged not to simply fill a middle-management role, but to step up to lead as the "chief missional strategist" or "keeper of the vision."

Six years ago, we introduced group coaching to the process of training. During the week of training, the coaches meet four times with their groups to provide space to process the didactic learning, foster peer connections at a deeper level, and receive coaching around the life transition that accompanies this new position.

Following that week of training, the groups (led by their coach) continue to meet monthly by video conference to discuss the changes occurring in their lives. The groups discuss strategies to forward inclusiveness in the church, process how to deal with conflict well, and identify best practices for engaging with their new judicatory peers.

13

TEAM COACHING

The first thing to realize about coaching a team of pastors is that a team is fundamentally different from a group. Groups come together for sharing and learning and then apply that learning to their individual settings outside the group. There is no shared group vision or set of group goals.

A team differs from a group in that the team establishes a shared vision as well as team goals, and the team rises or falls together because of their shared responsibility for results produced.

A team has a shared vision as well as established team goals.

Consider this comparison. Five middle school students meet to talk about the individual book reports they will each give in class at the end of the week. They are each responsible for their own book report. They share ideas and learn from one another, but beyond that there is no shared outcome or accountability. Each student will receive an individual grade on his or her report. This is a group.

Compare that with five students assigned by their teacher to work together to complete a research project. Their common purpose is to produce a single product to which they each contribute. In the end, team members will all receive the same grade based on their collaborative work. This is a team.

Here is coach Ginger Cockerham's definition of team coaching.

> Team Coaching is a facilitated process where participants are enrolled by a team leader for a specific intention related to accomplishing goals or milestones. A team with a coaching approach is focused on the team's overall win and what it takes for each individual to contribute to the team's win.[1]

Team in the Congregational Setting

A question worth considering is whether the administrative bodies leading congregations are teams or groups. Are members of the vestry or administrative council or session committed first to the overarching congregational goals, more so than to their individual committee interests and responsibilities? Is there a willingness to sacrifice individual desires and budgets for the greater good of the congregation?

Too often silo forming, protectionism, and competition describe the functioning of church-governing bodies. A first major challenge of congregational team coaching is to help church leadership move from simply existing as a group to functioning as a team.

A first major challenge of congregational team coaching is to help church leadership move … to functioning as a team.

In his book *Coaching Change*, Tom Bandy writes,

> The biggest mental shift in the postmodern world is that church leaders need to stop longing for institutional renewal and start working to rebuild the team. The next biggest shift is that church leaders need to recognize that their situation is more like amateur sports than professional sports. Although rebuilding the team might mean replacing the coach, trading older players away, or drafting new talent, the reality in amateur sports is: the coach you have is as good as you can get, the players you have are the ones who show up, the talent you want is already there—just buried.[2]

Importance of Purpose

The existence of a compelling purpose is the most critical component of a well-functioning team. A church devoted to the full inclusion of everyone and committed to standing against every form of injustice has a compelling purpose. The church dedicated to saving every lost soul who does not know Christ so they do not perish in hell also has a compelling purpose. Not every church will embrace the same purpose, but having a vibrant purpose is the essential element.

The existence of a compelling purpose is the most critical component of a well-functioning team.

Too often mainline churches are either not clear about their purpose or have strayed a great distance from it. Original clarity about why the congregation exists has been replaced with the *de facto* ambition of "getting more people to attend church so the church can pay its bills and not go out of existence." This reactive purpose is not persuasive enough to marshal a team's deepest convictions and passions or attract new members.

Even though many denominations have lifted up an overall purpose for all their congregations, such as "making disciples," many congregations struggle with exactly what that looks like for them.

Forming a Team

An artful coach will work first with the organizers of a team to make sure the purpose for creating the team is clear and captivating. If it is not, the coach will push for greater clarity by asking questions like, "How will the organization be decidedly different because this team was formed?" and "What calling is this team fulfilling?"

In addition to a compelling purpose, the coach works with the organizing leaders ahead of time to make sure these other essential factors are in place:

- The composition of the team makes sense and is clearly defined.
- The right people are on the team for the right reasons (stakeholders).
- The team has the support of the organization's leadership, including adequate funding, and is given enough authority to make meaningful change.
- The team has a solid structure, including clear, meaningful details of what is required of team members, administrative

support, agreeable meeting times, and a reasonable timeline.

Research on group coaching tells us that those four factors along with a compelling purpose account for 60 percent of the chance that the team will be successful. The other 40 percent of the team's chance of succeeding hinges on the coaching provided to the team.[3]

If you have ever painted a room in your house, you know that at least 60 percent of the work is in the preparation, such as taping off woodwork, patching holes, and sanding walls. The least of the undertaking is applying paint to the wall. The careful advanced work most governs the outcome. This same principle is true in forming a team.

Coaching a Team

After a team is adequately formed, the coach works with the team to develop a covenant. This is basically the list of ground rules for how the team will operate and interact, and covers topics such as confidentiality, respectful communication, expectations, levels of commitment, and common understanding of purpose. It is critical to form such an alliance at the very beginning so the team can refer back to it as team members work together. Actually, developing this covenant becomes a team effort in itself and requires full participation and consensus among members of the team.

One thing even highly productive teams have in common is that they don't spend much time in self-reflection. Teams just get busy doing what they were formed to do, rarely asking questions like, "Are all the voices on the team being heard and honored?" "What happens to our teamwork when we are at our worst?" and "Who provides the energy for this team, and who are the energy suckers?"

One place a coach can be utilized is helping a team identify its dynamics; the coach can then assist the team in making adjustments. The coach is a neutral voice outside the team who can ask discerning questions about how the team functions. A team coach helps the team clarify and focus on being purpose-driven, and also helps team members align interactions to support that purpose. The coach helps the team become a collection of reflective practitioners.

The coach is a neutral voice outside the team who can ask discerning questions about how the team functions.

Coaches also help teams dream bigger and expand possibilities. This is especially appropriate in the visioning or brainstorming phase of teamwork. We help the team think broadly about untapped potential and emerging opportunities. Teams sometimes need help in stretching to imagine the outrageous, so we ask questions such as, "In your wildest imagination, what is possible here?" and "What goal could this team set that would knock your socks off?"

Another role in coaching a team is for the coach to push the team toward action, especially with a team that tends to spend more time talking about what needs to occur than actually making things happen. At this point the coach can suggest that the team make a list of written action items. Before a meeting ends, the coach asks what, who, and when questions, such as, "What is the first action step?" "Who on the team is responsible for getting it done?" and "By when will it be completed?"

Organizational Development Consultants

In my experience as a coach, I have not often been hired to assist a team through the important work described above. Organizational development consultants are more likely to have an opportunity to do this work within an organization, utilizing team coaching along with their overall skillset of administering assessments, evaluating operations, and making recommendations for improvement.

As we have discussed earlier, coaching is a different modality than consulting, primarily resting upon a different understanding about with whom the expertise lies. However, some of the best organizational consultants adroitly make use of coaching for portions of their work. And many of them do this very well.

Some of the best organizational consultants adroitly make use of coaching for portions of their work.

Notes

1. Ginger Cockerham, *Group Coaching: A Comprehensive Blueprint* (Bloomington, IN: iUniverse, 2011), 2.
2. Thomas G. Bandy, *Coaching Change*, (Nashville, TN: Abingdon Press, 2000), 70.
3. J. Richard Hackman, "Six Common Misperceptions about Teamwork," *Harvard Business Review*, June 7, 2011, https://hbr.org/2011/06/six-common-misperceptions-abou?utm_source=feedburner.

14

COACHING NEW FAITH COMMUNITIES

Even existing churches that view themselves as friendly and welcoming develop norms and traditions that over time become part of their DNA, and in doing so, unwittingly create a closed system with a steep curve of assimilation for new members. Freshly emerging faith communities attract new disciples in greater numbers than existing congregations.

This is why over the last twenty to thirty years, most denominations have invested a great deal of focus, time, and money planting churches and birthing new faith communities. The virtuous motivation for this effort has been the opportunity to share the Good News of Jesus Christ with more people; the more utilitarian incentive has been to try to offset the precipitous membership decline in existing churches by planting new congregations.

Freshly emerging faith communities attract new disciples in greater numbers than existing congregations.

The initiative to plant new faith communities has met with varying degrees of success, but having a coach seems to be a common denominator among those that have succeeded. In the realm of ministry, denominations that have put coaching systems in place have seen their church-planting success rates increase dramatically.

A 2004 study conducted in the Four Square denomination showed that

> Two-thirds of church planters had the benefit of a coach as part of their church-planting experience. Of those who were coached, 77 percent reported that coaching had "some" to "very significant" impact on their personal effectiveness and productivity, with 54 percent reporting coaching had "significant" or "very significant" influence.[1]

One church planter says, "I know this—I've planted a church without a coach, and I've planted a church with a coach. All I can tell you is that I'll never plant a church without a coach again."[2]

In the highly innovative endeavor of birthing a new faith community, the coach becomes a critical thinking partner, providing much needed ongoing support and encouragement in what can be lonely and frustrating labor. Some coaches work only with the pastor planting the church; others coach the pastor and the core team. The coaching relationship may be utilized at one or all of the stages of planting: exploration, development, implementation, and leader development.

RUMINATION

Rev. Jesus Reyes, canon to the ordinary for congregational development, the Episcopal Diocese of El Camino Real.

Church planting is lonely work, especially at first, for two reasons. First, planters often break up the myths about church growth by finding fresh ways to reach new disciples, which is sometimes threatening to established churches that are not attracting new disciples. Secondly, there is a lot of work to accomplish in starting a congregation, and planters often overextend themselves by taking on too much themselves.

A coach can help a planter by bringing a point of reference about what is realistic so the planter doesn't lose track of reality. Coaching provides a level of reflection to balance the highly intuitive and entrepreneurial work of starting a new faith community.

For many years, a basic assumption in this field of coaching was that the best coach for a new church start is a coach who has also had the experience of starting a new church. While the inherent benefits based on this assumption may be obvious, the fact that what used to work rarely works now dissipates the impact of that familiarity. An experienced planter who now coaches newer planters must be sure to honor the very different context of the new plant because the needs will be altogether novel. Some of the best of church plants have both a consultant acting as a subject matter expert and a coach who can just coach.

The Role of Coaching

Here are some of the essential roles played by the coach during the church planning process.

- Chief Encourager, especially when things get rough for the pastor.
- Shoulder to Whine on, the coach provides a safe place to talk about frustrations and doubts.

- Wisdom Broker, sometimes planter coaches were/are also planters.
- Reminder, because planting is such demanding and stressful work it is easy for the pastor to lose sight of other parts of their life, like family.
- Prodder, the coach dares to get pushy about actions and to ask the tough questions.
- Accountability partner, planter coaches provide crucial accountability and tracking structures to help keep the planting process on task and moving forward.

Distinctions of Planter Coaching

One distinction in this type of coaching is that very often the coaching sessions are scheduled frequently, sometimes weekly, because of the rate at which plans must be set and evaluated and revised. It is also common for the coaching relationship to span one to three years or the duration of the church plant, rather than a season of several months which is more common in other forms of leadership coaching.

An additional distinction about this coaching is that the focus for every coaching session does not always come from the person being coached. As explained in Chapter 12, some of the conversations are "content-full," meaning the coach initiates the focus of the discussion around certain benchmarks that must be met by certain dates, or according to best practices in church planting.

A common trap for church planters is to get so involved in the process of planting a church that actually developing and launching the church becomes the end goal. Biblically, the objective of every congregation is to make disciples of Jesus. That objective holds true for new congregations that are being developed. The grand intention is to spread faith in Jesus Christ, not starting one more congregation. It is helpful for the individuals coaching the leaders who are establishing new faith communities to remind the planters of that intention from time to time.

Another two themes planter coaches return to on a regular basis are vision and purpose. These concepts are so essential to congregational development that they must continuously shine like the headlights of all the efforts to establish a new faith community. When one or both of these headlights become dim, the church plant is in trouble. Because the vision and purpose can and must adapt over time, it is the role of the coach to continue to ask the questions, "What is your vision?" and "What is the purpose of this faith community?"

The Role of the Coach When a New Church Initiative Fails

Honestly, planting churches is risky business, and not all attempts to start new congregations are successful. Because there are so many volatile components in starting a new faith community, the role of the coach is to help the leadership discern reasons for a breakdown. What matters is harvesting what can be learned from the experiment as a way of informing future efforts, rather than assigning blame. It is often the planter coach, who has accompanied the leadership all along the way, who can most effectively lead this process of review.

A Different Breed of Planters

There used to be a stereotype of what a successful church planter looked like. The successful planter was white, male, young and good looking with a sweet wife and small children. Of course, this pastor had to possess many additional substantive personality and leadership attributes typical of church planters, but for many years this ideal was defining.

In the last two years, I have been supervising coaches of church planters, or sometimes now called "mission developers," in two denominations that experienced a mass exodus of emblematic church planters more than a decade ago when the denominations voted to become fully inclusive of persons of different sexual orientations.

Suddenly, most of the pastors who fit the conventional profile of successful church planters had transferred to independent congregational systems. What emerged in the vacuum was an amazingly eclectic group of Generation X and millennial pastors with a fervent call to reach new disciples. And they look nothing like the previous formulaic stereotype! They are very young, extremely passionate, sometimes tattooed or pierced, and willing to risk it all for the sake of sharing the Good News. They are birthing new faith communities from food trucks, coffee shops, bars, and night clubs. One pastor leads a congregation that has no standard meeting place; she simply texts her congregation about worshiping times and places such as the park or the state fair. The congregation appears, flash-mob style.

This new generation of innovative congregational developers requires a different kind of coach. A graying coach who started a church back in 1990 might not be the best fit for these new planters, unless that coach is able to relinquish his or her attachment to the way things were and bring a beginner's mind to a whole new societal context.

Notes

1. Steve Ogne and Tim Roehl, *TransforMissional Coaching: Empowering Leaders in a Changing Ministry World* (Nashville, TN), B&H Publishing Group, 2008), 81.
2. Steve Ogne and Tim Roehl, *TransforMissional Coaching:*

Empowering Leaders in a Changing Ministry World,
(Nashville, TN), B&H Publishing Group, 2008), 25.

15

COACHING THROUGH
CONGREGATIONAL CONFLICT

Congregational conflict is on the rise, in part because of the degree of frustration many churches feel as they grow smaller, cut budgets, and face the difficult reality that their attractional appeal in society is diminishing. Division around values and social issues also contributes to the tensions and sensitivities that people bring with them to church, which makes it difficult for clergy to remain neutral or non-political.

In this charged environment, coaching can help congregations from getting to the point of serious divisional conflict by facilitating healthy processes and decision-making that honors all voices and emphasizes respectful communication. Very often, pastors who are leading their congregations into a season of potentially divisive challenges can work with a coach to envision how the process might play out and design a process that is both equitable and reverential. What matters most is not what a congregation ends up deciding, but how they treat one another in the process of deciding.

> What matters most is not what a congregation ends up deciding, but how they treat one another.

Coaching Skills Used During Conflict Transformation

Most congregations effectively handle low-level conflict. In fact, this level of conflict is an expected part of the healthy process of being in ministry, adapting programs, addressing social needs, or making change. A coach can be very helpful to a pastor or congregational leader who is in the midst of low-level conflict by providing a safe place for thoughtful reflection, exploration of possibilities, and consideration of action steps.

However, in situations of high-level conflict, it is wise to consider engaging the help of a skilled conflict transformation consultant. The term *conflict resolution* is frequently used, but we prefer the term *conflict transformation* because under God's influence, conflict can be a point of reordering and bringing about needed change. A transformational consultant would be helpful at times when congregational conflict has taken the form of individuals choosing sides or demonizing their opponents, and the outcome has become win or lose. At its worst, the chairs are flying.

The consultant may physically come on-site to meet with the principals involved in the conflict, do some teaching, and help design steps toward resolution. A different approach the consultant may take is to use the skills of coaching to work behind the scenes with the pastor and perhaps other key leaders to help them find a way forward in resolving their own conflict.

RUMINATION

Dr. W. Craig Gilliam, executive director of Gilliam and Associates, LLC, works with the Center for Leadership/Pastoral

Excellence for the Louisiana Conference, consults/facilitates with Just Peace Center for Mediation and Conflict Transformation, is an adjunct at Perkins School of Theology, SMU, and is a Gallup-Certified Strengths Coach

We call this work "conflict transformation" rather than "conflict resolution" because there is rarely resolution to church conflict, especially on the deeper, more adaptive issues that happen on the level of emotional processing. Transformation is deeper than resolution, and even deeper than transformation is our own biblical model of reconciliation.

Transformation is foundational work that has systemic as well as individual components. We work with congregations at the systemic level because that seems to have more lasting results than just moving the chess players around the chessboard. Without the deeper systemic work, tomorrow the same congregation may be dealing with another identified issue while the emotional process is still the same. We seek not to change the players but to change the culture or environment they are working in.

The coaching skills of deep listening, good questions, curiosity, and direct communication are all helpful in my work with congregations in conflict. While some of the skills of coaching are utilized in conflict transformation, coaching and conflict transformation are not the same. The system work of conflict transformation has its own skill set.

Truly, journeying with congregations through conflict to transformation is more about art than it is about science. We follow certain principles, some of which are similar to coaching, but most of this work is the work of an artist.

"Transformation is deeper than resolution, and even deeper than transformation is our own biblical model of reconciliation."

DR. CRAIG GILLIAM

Coaching Following Conflict

After successfully moving through a season of conflict, there is a ripe time to engage a coach to help leaders process and learn from what happened. When the heat of conflict is finally dialed down, it is time to ask, "What does God intend for me/us to learn? What needs to be different? What is next?"

Here are some of the guiding principles in coaching leaders following conflict:

- As a congregation moves successfully through a time of highly charged struggle, there is a capricious opening for both individual and organizational transformation.
- Deep healing is possible even when members of a congregation have chosen sides and hurt one another because God is always restoring God's creation. The work of coaching in the aftermath of conflict is restorative and hopeful work that knows no limits.
- The coach should support the leader in reflecting on what led to the conflict as a way to learn from this experience. This effort should be approached much like performing an autopsy. This kind of critical evaluation cannot come from

the leader's head alone; it requires the soul, intuition, and the guidance of the Holy Spirit.

- Church leaders need support as they do the courageous work of self-examination, but they also need accountability. The role of the coach is to provide both.
- The most challenging part of this work is helping a leader "own" his or her part in the conflict. Often it is in the naming or the "saying out loud" that leaders are freed and can find a way forward.

There is a capricious opening for both individual and organizational transformation.

RUMINATION

Dr. Karin Walker, associate certified coach, lead pastor of Falston United Methodist Church, former district superintendent of the Baltimore Suburban District in the Baltimore-Washington Conference of the United Methodist Church

A coach may begin working with the pastor in terms of helping her/him understand the style of conflict resolution that comes naturally. There are several resources that can further information around styles of conflict, but specifically helping a pastor realize and identify patterns of response in the midst of conflict can shape his or her further response in the current situation.

For example, a pastor who is fearful of conflict and retreats in the midst of it may give the impression of being indifferent or impotent, allowing for the conflicted party to bully forward. Or a pastor who responds aggressively in the mist of conflict can potentially scare away (literally) the principals and lose them to the faith community altogether. A coach can come alongside a pastor or key leaders and work with them to assess their responses and proactively plan an approach that will garner the best results. Given that none of us is at our best in the midst of conflict, coaching through the conflict helps clients understand their current status and helps them intentionally plan the desired outcome.

Coaching is an invaluable tool in helping congregational leaders design processes to minimize polarization in conflict, move all the way through congregational conflict to transformation, and learn from the experience. The aim of all coaching is "to evoke transformation"; in the church we know this is nothing short of holy work borne of sacred imagination that can lead to God-sized outcomes.

EPILOGUE

Conference and judicatory leaders have been investing in clergy leadership by hiring ICF certified coaches, developing clergy peer coaching networks, or training internal coaches to help leaders grow and improve in effectiveness. One conference trained their entire Board of Ordained Ministry, and they reported it was the best use of their development budget.

But the conferences and middle judicatories that are paying for this coaching and coach training are now rightfully asking about the valuation of their return on investment. In other words, what difference is the investment of time and money in coaching making?

What difference is the investment of time and money in coaching making?

What Is ROI?

In brief, the business formula for calculating the return on investment (ROI) involves subtracting the costs of coaching from the estimated value of the outcomes of coaching and then expressing this as a percentage.

For example, GlaxoSmithKline (GSK), winner of the 2016 ICF International Prism Award, created a global Coaching Centre of Excellence that standardized coaching throughout the organization by improving access, ensuring quality and efficiency, and creatively containing costs. Coaching at GSK has increased by 2,900 percent within the last half-decade and has been credited with an ROI of $66 million USD.[1] The GSK ROI dollar values are based on improvements in productivity, innovation, reductions in costs, retention of high performers, and other leading indicators of profitability.

Google's Way of Measuring

The simplest way to measure the value of coaching is to survey those who have been coached, asking them to rate the value they have received from coaching. It can be as simple as asking, "On a scale of one to five, what value have you received from coaching?"

The simplest way to measure the value of coaching is to survey those who have been coached.

Google evaluates the ROI of coaching in terms of what employees perceive as their most valuable resource: time. In other words, they measure the benefits of coaching based on whether employees see coaching as a valuable use of their time. After working with an internal coach, Google employees provide an average rating of 4.8 out of 5, with 5 being the most valuable use of their time.

Employees of Google who have received coaching cite a host of positive benefits, including accelerated onboarding, increased self-confidence, and enhanced executive presence.[2]

What ICF Research Measures

Conducted in partnership between the Human Capital Institute (HCI) and as reported by more than 500 professionals, a signature research study by the International Coach Federation (ICF) investigated the components of a successful coaching culture as well as the state of coaching within secular organizations.

What the study found is that 65 percent of employees are highly engaged in strong coaching culture organizations compared to 52 percent of employees in other organizations. Organizations with a strong coaching culture also report greater financial performance: 60 percent report being above their industry peer group in 2013 revenue compared to 41 percent of all others.

Coaching is used in organizations as a leadership development strategy, to increase employee engagement, to improve communication and teamwork skills, and to increase productivity. With more organizations recognizing the importance of coaching, 80 percent report that, within the next five years, they expect that managers/leaders will expand their use of coaching skills. While most organizations report that senior-level (80 percent) and high-potential employees (87 percent) receive coaching, more than 60 percent report that entry-level employees receive some amount of coaching as well.[3]

Is ROI an Appropriate Measure for Clergy Coaching?

The top four areas measured by ROI in the business world are increased efficiency, improved revenue, employee retention, and productivity. I have yet to coach a pastor who indicates at the outset of coaching that he or she wants to improve efficiency, revenue, retention, or productivity. However, some of the improvements clergy do seek from coaching fall into these areas while using different language. Here are the clergy corollaries to each of those areas.

- Increased efficiency = Better time management and boundary setting.
- Improved revenue = Growth in congregational giving to support the church budget or capital campaign.
- Employee retention = Volunteer engagement and spiritual growth of disciples.
- Productivity = Accomplishing strategic goals and meeting growth objectives.

Many denominations track a handful of congregational measures reported by congregations each year, thereby establishing patterns in a congregation's overall growth or decline. That data has been used to measure "church vitality," with significant pushback from congregations for tying numerical data so closely to the notion of vitality.

Because congregations are not-for-profit organizations, it is difficult to compare investment against profit. Obviously, other measures must be taken into account. But what are the right measures? Average worship attendance, new professions of faith, increase in stewardship? Or congregational engagement in change, missional efforts to reach the surrounding community, the deepening of discipleship through small groups? Should we measure the through puts or the outputs? Are the leading indicators of qualitative development and quantitative growth the same?

Should we measure the through puts or the outputs?

Anthony M. Grant, coeditor of *The Evidence Based Coaching Handbook: Putting Best Practices to Work for Your Clients,* argues that ROI is a poor measure of coaching success in any organization. He makes the case for a more holistic approach using a well-being and engagement framework.

> The research clearly shows that coaching has great potential to enhance the performance, productivity and well-being of individuals, organizations and the people that work for them. Organizations and workplaces are more than just money-making machines. They are social and psychological contexts in which people live, work, and relate. Of course, money-making is important. But so is the development, growth and well-being of the people that constitute organizations and workplaces. We do our clients, ourselves, and the coaching industry a great disservice by overly focusing on the financial outcomes of coaching.[4]

"We do our clients, ourselves and the coaching industry a great disservice by overly focusing on the financial outcomes of coaching."

—ANTHONY M. GRANT

RUMINATION

Dr. George (Skip) Casey, professional certified coach, applied anthropology and human organization specialist

The Church needs to identify two important categories of measurements to effectively evaluate the ROI of coaching and to fulfill its potential. Those two categories are leading indicators and trailing indicators. The measurements currently being used to identify vital churches are trailing indicators.

Trailing indicators are quantitative outcomes and results like attendance, increases in membership, baptisms, giving, small groups, and participation in missions. The vital questions are: What qualitative leading indicators produce those results? What are the qualities of a congregation, lay leadership, and clergy leadership that produce those outcomes? Are those qualities the same in every context? Is there just one purpose for every congregation in a variety of contexts? Effective measurements of coaching ROI must be valid and reliable measurements of the leading indicators that produce the quantitative trailing indicators of success. Those leading indicators may include:

How attractive and compelling is the stated purpose of the local congregation?

How well are productive healthy values being identified, modeled, and practiced?

How effectively are processes and policies being refined and applied?

What is the right leadership for this congregation's purpose?

How well are lay leaders being identified, recruited, developed, and engaged?

The leading indicators may vary with the difference in contexts, purposes, and people. An effective coaching culture will continually discover, measure, and develop the qualitative leading indicators that produce the trailing indicators needed for each church's purpose.

This will require a change in executive church leadership and culture. The effectiveness of coaching cannot be separated from the context in which it is working. Coaching is most effective in adaptive learning organizations.

Research Findings from Discipleship Ministries

In 2008, the Orientation Design Team for new middle-level judicatory leaders in the United Methodist Church decided to augment the orientation process by offering on-site group coaching, followed by four months of continued group coaching by phone. This addition of coaching was well received and has consistently been ranked highest in the evaluations completed by participants. Until 2016, our conclusions concerning the effectiveness of the coaching were only anecdotal.

The Research Department of the General Board of Discipleship of the United Methodist Church released a study in June 2016 validating the effect this coaching was having on the 2015 attendees. The study found some leaders felt better prepared and adjusted to their new role than others. The causal factor between these two groups was the degree to which the leader participated in the follow-up coaching provided after the orientation.

Those who took full advantage of the coaching were less stressed and anxious, more confident, felt their knowledge was sufficient for their work, and felt more qualified and prepared for their job.

> **Those who took full advantage of the coaching were less stressed and anxious ... and felt more qualified and prepared for their job.**

For all outcomes but one, those respondents who engaged in a higher level of coaching saw their outcomes improve after the post-event survey. In contrast, for all outcomes but two, those respondents who engaged in a lower level of coaching saw their outcomes worsen after the post-event survey.[5]

The research confirmed empirically what before we had only known intuitively.

What Is Still Needed

A reliable tool has yet to be developed for universally measuring the return on investment in coaching clergy. What is needed is a research-proven instrument that would measure not just the subjective indicators of the effectiveness of coaching such as "satisfaction of those being coached," but also objective measures of the empirical outcomes of the coaching.

Suffice it to say, we still have a way to go in the field of coaching to determine with more accuracy the ROI of coaching clergy.

Notes

1. International Coaching Federation Prism Award, "Creating a Coaching Culture for Better Talent," last accessed March 21, 2018, https://coachfederation.org/app/uploads/2017/10/CaseStudy_GSK.pdf
2. Case study Google and Executive Coaching, C. B. Bowman,

last accessed April 25, 2018,
https://www.slideshare.net/princessslattie/case-study-
google-and-executive-coaching.

3. Executive Summary, Human Capital Institute with The
   International Coach Federation, "Building a Coaching
   Culture," last accessed March 21, 2018,
   http://www.hci.org/hr-research/building-coaching-
   culture.

4. Anthony M. Grant, "ROI is a poor measure of coaching
   success: Towards a more holistic approach using a well-
   being and engagement framework," Coaching: An
   International Journal of Theory, Research and Practice 2012.
   1–12, iFirst article last accessed March 28, 2018,
   http://researchportal.coachfederation.org/MediaStream/
   PartialView?documentId=532.

5. The Research Department of the General Board of
   Discipleship of the United Methodist Church shared these
   results internally with staff of the General Board of
   Discipleship in June 2016.

APPENDIX

Coach Approach Skill Training (CAST) is the coach training created in 2007 by George Howard and Chris Holmes at the request of the General Board of Discipleship of the United Methodist Church. This "professional grade" education, approved by the International Coach Federation, leads to credentialing as a coach and is now one of the largest coach skills training programs specifically targeted to clergy and laity in the United States. In 2016, training began globally in parts of Europe and Africa.

CAST is also one of the most affordable coach trainings currently available on the market. Keeping this training affordable is an intentional decision to spread the skills of coaching as far and wide as possible at all levels of the Christian church.

The curriculum for the sixty hours of coach training concentrates on the eleven core competencies of coaching in a format that is highly engaging and widely participatory.

Coach
Approach
Skill
Training

COACH APPROACH SKILL TRAINING CONTENT OVERVIEW

CAST 1: The Basics

15 hours of coach-specific training

Over two days, participants learn the five basic skills of coaching and come away with a ministry plan for how to use those skills in their ministry. The course covers the history and benefits of coaching, establishing a contact, importance of presence, deep listening, asking powerful questions, expanding possibilities, action planning, and review and commitment.

CAST 2: Advanced Skills

15 hours of coach-specific training

This two-day training deepens the basic skills while introducing the advanced skills of coaching to denominational leaders and pastors and laypeople working to build vital congregations. The training covers direct communication, hunches and blurts and blunders, encouragement and celebration, huge requests and challenges, metaphors and image, and saboteur and future self.

CAST 3: Group and Team Coaching

15 hours of coach-specific training

Coaching a group or a team is a specialized skill requiring the ability to combine group facilitation with coaching. Covered in this two-day course are: the difference between a team and a group, stages of team life, establishing a team, the art of team coaching, the third entity, reading system intelligence, and the benefits and special challenges of group coaching.

CAST 4: Synergy

15 hours of coach-specific training

In a series of eight TeleClasses, students dive deeper into the understanding of appreciative coaching, the spirituality of coaching, the art of coaching, ICF core competencies and code of ethics, and several coaching practicums. Each synergy class is led live by an instructor, is conducted by internet video, and lasts two hours.

The CAST learning experience is highly participatory with heavy emphasis on the integration and practice of the core competencies of coaching. It provides the necessary hours of coach-specific training required by the International Coach Federation and includes 150 pages of written instructional material. The CAST Fast Track training occurs over a four-month period as a combination of homework, webinars, and one week of in-person training. CAST modules can also be taken as separate two-day seminars spread out over time. We hold our trainings on-site in various locations in the US and abroad. For more information about this training go to www.holmescoaching.com.

ACKNOWLEDGMENTS

How marvelous it is to have the opportunity to lift up the main contributors in this coaching endeavor … my parents, Bill and Nancy Holmes, for eight decades of helpful life coaching … Bishop John Schol, who first sent me to be trained as a coach … Coaches Training Institute, which provided wonderful training … Ron Renaud from CTI, who modeled great teaching … my Sacred Fire buddies Rod Miller, Larry Ousley, and Jim Robey, who fanned the flames … George Howard, my co-creator, friend, and brother … Susan Ruach and Vance Ross, who launched my very first training sessions … United Methodist Bishop Bill McAlilly and Episcopal Bishop Scott Benhase, two dear friends who believed in me early on and trusted me to coach their clergy … my life mentor Jay Stearns and the Men's Group that he leads who have sustained my passion for over twenty years… Skip Casey, Chris Owens, Youngsook Kang, Karin Walker, Walter Hobgood, William Chaney, Owen Ross, Anne Kiome, Marti Soper, and Vicki Loflin Johnson, with whom I am privileged to teach … the Auburn Seminary coaching faculty— Laurie Ferguson and Phil Bergey … Gayle Irvin with whom I teach in Scotland … the wonderful affiliate coaches who are part of the

Holmes Coaching Group ... the Maryland Chapter of the ICF who elected me as their president ... Lynda Otte, the behind-the-scenes executive assistant who is a person of rich faith and who is worth her weight in gold.

I am especially grateful for these nineteen leaders and coaches who have contributed immensely by sharing their ruminations in this book: Drew Dyson, Wanda Duckett, Rodney Smothers, Dede Roberts, Claire Bowen, Aaron Bouwens, Vicki Loflin Johnson, Varlyna Wright, Youngsook Charlene Kang, Stephen Coburn, Scott Benhase, Myrna Bethke, Brian Brown, Arun Paul, Whitney Mitchell, Jesus Reyes, Craig Gilliam, Karin Walker, and George (Skip) Casey.

I am also deeply grateful for each pastor, layperson, and church leader who leaned into the coaching relationship with me so God could work the magic.

ABOUT THE AUTHOR

While serving in a middle-judicatory role as a district superintendent in the Baltimore-Washington Conference of the United
Methodist Church, Chris registered for training with the world's
largest in-person coach training organization, the Coaches Training
Institute. He ended the training two years later with a vision for
how these powerful coaching skills could make a huge difference
when applied to the context of ministry. Since then, Chris has been
meeting the growing appetite among clergy and denominational
leaders to learn the basic skills of coaching as a response to clergy
isolation and to lead with the coach approach to ministry as a form
of empowerment. Feeding that hunger at every level of the church
and in all Christian denominations is now his calling and life work.

Over the past ten years, Chris has trained and mentored thousands
of pastors and leaders in the skill set and mindset of coaching for
ministry in every part of the United States as well as Africa University in Zimbabwe and the Church of Scotland. Those pastors and
leaders represent several Christian denominations and secular
universities, including Auburn Seminary.

The Holmes Coaching Group, led by Chris, is made up of twelve
ICF-accredited affiliate coaches working broadly in several Christian denominations. In 2018, Chris launched the "Academy of
Artful Leadership," partnering with over thirty trained coaches to
provide group and team coaching to hundreds of pastors and
laypeople across the United States.

Chris is accredited as a professional coach by the International Coach Federation. He is a founding member of the Maryland Chapter of the ICF and a past-president of that organization. He is also an accomplished watercolor artist, husband to Margaret, and father to three grown children—Lindsey, Jenny, and Taylor.

Made in the USA
Middletown, DE
23 January 2019